# Confronting the
# Idolatry of Family

# Confronting the Idolatry of Family

## A New Vision for the Household of God

# Janet Fishburn

Abingdon Press
Nashville

CONFRONTING THE IDOLATRY OF FAMILY:
A New Vision for the Household of God

*Copyright © 1991 by Abingdon Press*

*This book is printed on acid-free paper.*

**Library of Congress Cataloging-in-Publication Data**

Fishburn, Janet Forsythe, 1937–
    Confronting the idolatry of family: a new vision for the household of God/Janet F. Fishburn.
        p.   cm.
    Includes bibliographical references.
    **ISBN 0-687-09401-1** (alk. paper)
    1. Church work with families—United States—Controversial literature. 2. Church renewal—United States. 3. United States—Church history—20th century. 4. Pastoral theology. 5. Protestant church—Doctrines. 6. Family—Biblical teaching. 7. Family—United States—Religious life. I. Title.
    BV4438.F57   1991
    261.8'3585'0973—dc20                                           90-26642
                                                                          CIP

Scripture quotations are from the New Revised Standard Version of the Bible, copyright © 1989, by the Division of Christian Education of the National Council of Churches of Christ in the United States of America.

MANUFACTURED IN THE UNITED STATES OF AMERICA

*With Gratitude*

# ACKNOWLEDGMENTS

This book comes from personal experience, my research and teaching, and from lifelong participation in Christian congregations. I am grateful to those congregations for teaching me what I know about membership in the household of God. Much of the "new vision" described in part 3 was learned from members of Diakonia, a congregation where most members are engaged in mutual ministry and in outreach ministries in their community.

Much of what I know about ministry comes from friends who are gifted pastors and from my students. I owe a special thanks to Art Hagy, who read the first draft, and Stanley Hauerwas, who read the last draft of this book. Art told me what I had to say of importance to pastors. Stanley was generous with appreciation and constructive criticism of my practical theology.

Much of what I know about families comes from being a daughter, a wife, and a mother. I am grateful to my daughters who freely discuss issues of their young-adult generation with me. I am deeply grateful to my husband, who enthusiastically supports my ministry.

Some books need a good editor more than others. This is one of them. It has not been easy to write about family idolatry while affirming the importance of family relationships to Christians. In Paul Franklyn and Sally Sharpe I have been blessed with the kind of editorial assistance I needed.

The Theological School
Drew University
Summer 1990

# CONTENTS

# Protestant Ideals and Historical Realities

This book is for pastors and Christian educators who wrestle with the difficult issue of how to include people from traditional and nontraditional families in the life of a congregation. My premise is that this is not possible unless those who lead congregations recognize that it is the church—and not a biological family unit—that is the first family of all baptized Christians. Since we become Christian as we participate in the life of a congregation, the way church leaders order the life and worship of a congregation is crucial to the spiritual well-being of all members of a congregation.

During the last twenty-five years, church leaders have experienced the impact of a major cultural transition on the life of congregations. A technological revolution and a changing economic order affect both church and family. Most congregations are affected by the changing family, membership loss, shrinking Sunday Schools, failure to retain youth, and a growing number of older members. The impact of a biomedical revolution raises new issues about sexual practices, the nature of conception and childbearing, and the meaning of marriage and parenthood. Even though these changes affect the daily life of all Christians, many pastors seem unable to lead a congregation in theological reflection about ethical issues.

My thesis is that Protestants in the United States are not yet fully aware of the extent to which the changing family affects the life of a congregation because our theologies, ministries, and traditions are influenced by a worldview that coalesced before the Civil War. Many people continue to think about sexuality, family, and church in ways that took shape in the Victorian era, a time of empire.

*Confronting the Idolatry of Family* challenges those who believe that "decline" in the family is the cause of moral decay in the nation and membership loss in churches. This perpetuates a belief held by pastors and theologians in the Victorian period that "the Christian family" was the building block of civilization without which neither nation nor children would be moral. This implies that the church exists primarily to support the moral fabric of the American democracy. During the Victorian era—approximately 1830–1913—an ultimacy was attributed to the formative power of "the Christian family." Protestants commonly regarded the family as "a little church."

Christianity has had a tendency to become a church of empire since the Constantinian era.[1] In 1971, historian Robert T. Handy argued that an American version of a church of empire was coming to an end. He referred to the transition then under way as a "second disestablishment of religion" in America. Handy suggested that since the Victorian period, Protestants had confused a civil religion—the hope of Christianizing America—with Christian faith. He pointed out that instead of the church having Christianized civilization, the Protestant churches in America had been domesticated.[2]

Although few Protestants would still claim that the United States is an "almost Christianized" nation, the Victorian way of thinking about the world, God, and human nature still influences theological discourse. The dualistic, or dichotomous, structure of Victorian thought is most evident in the way modern Protestants approach moral issues. The Victorian way of dividing the world into male and female roles and spheres still influences the way we organize the life of a congregation.

Members in the church today are commonly referred to as "private" or "public," "conservative" or "liberal." The public/

private dichotomy refers to assumptions about the role of the Protestant church in American culture. The conservative/liberal dichotomy refers most often to a stance on theological ethics and a way of using the Bible. The tone of disagreement, especially obvious with reference to sexuality, is that of the Victorian era. The Victorians had confidence in their own intellectual and moral righteousness, born of a philosophical assumption that truth is self-evident.

The church members find dialogue difficult because they rarely question their presuppositions about human nature or how truth is known.[3] Yet, these things are similar in many ways. Both assume a hierarchy of social values, moral values, and intellectual values that belong to the Protestant impulse associated with an American religion of empire.[4] I refer to this impulse as the *American Dream.*

Scholarly investigation of the differences between Protestant ideals and historical realities seems to have had little impact on the practice of ministry. The belief that America is—or ought to be—a Christian nation continues to subtly dominate the way many Protestants think about the life of a congregation. I am suggesting that it is not the mission of Protestant churches to make America Christian, or even to transform American culture. Further, we will not be free from family idolatry—the effect of attributing ultimacy to "the Christian family" on Protestant spirituality—unless we are free from illusions about "a Christian America."

The present situation of cultural transition and of perceived decline in churches is an opportunity for reflection about what it means to be Christian in a pluralistic culture. What does it mean to participate in "new life in Christ" for late-twentieth-century Christians? What does it mean to love Jesus Christ more than family?

*Confronting the Idolatry of Family* is divided into three sections. Part 1 is an analysis of the origins of current attitudes about church and family.

Part 2 is a discussion of the way values often believed to be "God-given and biblical" are related to the values of the American Dream. Some years ago James Smart observed that one of the reasons the Bible is "strangely silent" in congregations is because pastors are not able to bring a "critical" perspective on Scripture to bear on faith issues.[5] With that in mind, I have attempted to address a biblically informed theological reflection to the key issues raised by transition in culture, church, and family.

In recent years there has been much discussion about "faith development" and the role of church and family in the "faith formation" of children and youth. I have concluded that a "Sunday School and Church" approach to Christian education is an inadequate mode of spiritual formation for persons in contemporary culture.

In Part 3, I describe the role of church leaders in planning educational programs that are supportive of members of traditional and nontraditional families, but not dependent on "the Christian home" as the primary agency of Christian spiritual formation.

Every generation can learn faith anew in dialogue with Scripture, tradition, and experience. Although I believe that modern Christians can be instructed by biblical perspectives on church and family, I am not advocating a return to some earlier time when the church may seem to have been more faithful. My conviction is that we cannot be led into God's future if we are not aware of some of the ways we have been formed by our history.

# Confronting the
# Idolatry of Family

# PART ONE

# "The Family Pew" in Domesticated Congregations

# CHAPTER 1

# *"The Family Pew":*

## The Church in Domestic Captivity

Americans who came of age in the decade after the Second World War are deeply imbued with the values and moral commitments of the American Dream. Many have a vision of a time when Americans were good citizens who went to church, when fathers went to work every day, mothers stayed home and took care of the children, and children obeyed their parents. Men and women nurtured in Protestant churches during the flowering of the American Dream long for a return to a time when all Americans seemed to share their vision of good citizenship and family life. This was a time when the rhythms of life were ordered from week to week as family members gathered for worship in "the family pew." Pastors and church members of that era still associate a sense of well-being with church membership and "the family pew."

*Mr. Jones, Meet the Master* was a religious best seller in the post-war recovery period. The book was written by a Scottish Presbyterian called to be pastor of the New York Avenue Presbyterian Church in Washington, Peter Marshall. The sentiments of a sermon in *Mr. Jones, Meet the Master* titled "Keepers of the Springs" may sound hopelessly old-fashioned to anyone born after 1960. Yet, this reminder that "women come nearer to fulfilling their God-given function in the home than anywhere else" still quickens the hearts of church-going Americans whose understanding of the world was formed by the domestic values associated with "the family pew" after World War II.[1]

> Do not think me fanciful . . . too imaginative . . . or too extravagant in my language when I say that I think of women, and particularly of our mothers, as Keepers of the Springs. . . . There never has been a time when there was a greater need for Keepers of the Springs, or when there were more polluted springs to be cleansed. If the home fails, the country is doomed. The breakdown of home life and influence will mark the breakdown of the nation. If the Keepers of the Springs desert their posts or are unfaithful to their responsibilities, the future outlook of this country is black indeed.[2]

"Keepers of the Springs" was first published in 1949. The same sermon, with very few changes in content or language, could have been written in 1850 or 1950. The origin of "the family pew" as a sign of cultural well-being goes back to the decades before the Civil War, a time of cultural transition. The dream of a loving, happy, church-going family as the hope of a Christian nation emerged as part of the American Dream during a time of cultural stress in the early Victorian period. Then, as now, there were extensive changes in family life, in the social roles of men and women. And then, as now, the stability of the family unit was linked with the prosperity and well-being of the nation.[3]

Although it may seem obvious that the values of the "family pew" still set the agenda for conservative congregations today, those values retain considerable power in shaping the agendas of all congregations. It is a sign of the power of "the family pew" if the major source of new members is through the baptism and confirmation of children of members. "Family pew" commitments are central issues where most church program considerations relate to the needs of a family consisting of a mother, a father, and several children. Although members may no longer sanction the sexual ethics of earlier generations, congregations continue to act on those values through the way they organize their activities. The structure of programs in most Protestant congregations has changed very little since the early Victorian period.

For instance, there has never been a very secure place for single adults in "the family pew." There is a sense that "something is wrong" with adults who do not marry. An unstated expectation that adults should marry and have children is operative today in parental concern about the sexuality of teens and the failure of young adults to marry.

One of the most difficult ethical issues for adult church members continues to be that of the sexuality of unmarried young adults. Programs offered for singles often reflect the Victorian assumption that everyone should marry. The isolation of single persons or childless couples from adults who are married and have children perpetuates the Victorian way of ordering relationships in a congregation; they organized all church activities to give optimal support to their vision of the ideal Christian family: a father, a mother, and several children.[4]

Even though there are single-parent and blended families in most congregations today, many church members still imagine "the family pew" with a father, a mother, and several children there together on Sunday morning. If a congregation or its pastor visualize membership in terms of this kind of family ideal, it is a sign of a culturally accommodated, domesticated faith. An unexamined commitment of pastors and people to values of "the family pew" is keeping Protestant churches from being able to offer spiritual formation for people from traditional and nontraditional families.

The family is a mediating social institution, especially as it mediates social and moral values to children. But a family unit socializes into its own value system which may be more or less Christian in values learned by children from their parents. If the family unit is believed to be the primary source of Christian faith, as it was in Protestant churches of the Victorian period, then the Church becomes an adjunct socializer and ritualizer of family events.

As Sydney Callahan points out, a domesticated church inevitably tends to become conservative, class conscious, sexist, and ineffectual in the society at large. This is why the mission of the church in family religious education is at one and the same time to transcend and support the family.[5]

## The Family and the American Dream

In a congregation where members experience Christian faith as a way of living in the world, a pastor has succeeded in bridging the gap between being a church member and life in a secular society. This is usually done through compelling worship, faithful interpretation of Scripture in preaching, and attention to building community among members of the congregation. Research shows that a clear focus on community-building in the congregation is related to the extent to which laity are active in ministries in the congregation and beyond the congregation.

Pastors who know how to lead laity into ministry have at least two leadership characteristics in common: They talk about the presence of God in the ordinary situations of daily life, and they are able to structure the life of a congregation so that members are encouraged and able to give ministry to one another. This involves devising an organizational structure suitable to the congregation. This unique structure gives members opportunities to learn Christian faith by living it, talking about it, and giving it away. Obviously, this means that the pastor is not the only or even the primary caregiver in the congregation.

Such pastors model servant ministry. The service they perform is in guiding the life of the congregation so that laity are free to grow through their own ministry. A lay leader of a congregation where worship is the spiritual center of the life of the congregation—like the hub of a wheel—reported that her pastor's gifts in worship leadership and preaching are "unequaled." Another member said that the pastor encourages "members of a diverse congregation to work together, not to become like each other, but to live closer to the example of Jesus." It was said of the same man that, "He has a reputation for being able to delegate authority to lay leaders and staff members."[6]

This combination of high morale and high commitment to the ministry of all Christians is relatively rare. More pastors are able to generate excitement in worship than commitment to ministry among members. One of the reasons why it is so difficult to lead laity into ministry is that the dream of "a Christian America" influences the way people understand Christian identity.[7] "The family pew" in the sanctuary continues to symbolize a well-established Protestant ideal about the role of Christianity in American culture.

Colleen McDannell describes this view of Christianity as it functioned for Protestants between 1840 and 1900.

> Protestants, through domestic rituals, attempted to create a concept of "Christianity" which would link them together under one common moral canopy. The evangelical vision hoped to counter the trend toward pluralism in America with the idea of a unified "Christian" nation. Domestic Protestantism, which asserted the values of hard work, purity, individual morality, and patriotism, was the foundation of this vision. The values of the home stood as eternal truths, whereas denominational theologies appeared splintered and irrelevant. Family religion arose as a means of returning to "simple Bible truths" which made good citizens.[8]

For most of the twentieth century the churches of America have continued to convey these ideals. They were so common at the beginning of the twentieth century that politicians like Theodore Roosevelt could "preach" them in political campaigns.[9] Through contact with family units, churches have been expected to inculcate the moral integrity necessary for freedom in a democratic society.

Support for the values associated with "the Christian home" gave moral purpose to the church and a clear role to pastors as long as no one questioned the reality of the family ideal. Churches perpetuated the American Dream by teaching and reinforcing the ideals of "the Christian home" and Christian citizenship. It was not until the changing family had become an undeniable reality in the 1960s that the once normative "family pew" ethos began to disintegrate. This is when two versions of the role of the Church in American culture emerged, one conservative and one liberal.[10]

The vision of "a Christian America" was a source of meaning and motivation for the values associated with the American Dream until very recently. It still informs the purpose and commitments of many congregations. Belief in "a Christian America" is undiminished among more conservative Protestants, especially in the South and the Midwest. Ronald Reagan and George Bush were elected by people who believe in the family ideals of a Christian nation. Although liberal church leaders are critical of the moral values associated with the American Dream, they continue to act on a belief in the transformation of American culture by the Church. This, too, is part of the American Dream.

### Family Ideals After the Second World War

The changes experienced in American culture since 1960 can be interpreted, in part, as a decline in the power of the vision of "a Christian America" to provide meaning and motivation for middle-class life. Affirmations of national morality have been seriously challenged by events such as the civil rights movement and the war in Vietnam. Uncritical patriotism, family loyalty, church membership, lifelong marriage, and the place of women in the home are, for many Americans, no longer unquestioned loyalties. Yet these are the commitments symbolized by "the family pew."

Church members and leaders who came of age before or during the years of national optimism and economic expansion following the Second World War have a vision of the way the world ought to be that comes from their experience of "the family pew." "The family pew" was a symbol that all was well with the world again—America had triumphed over the evil powers of the world. Families were reunited. "Normal" family life resumed.

Victory in the war recalled for church-going Americans one

of the recurring motifs of American religion, the vision of "a Christian America." This motif dominated the nineteenth-century church, but it reemerges whenever the economy is strong and the white middle-class experiences relative security.[11] In the vision of "a Christian America," good citizens are good Christians who go to church. Good Christians have good families who go to church together. After the war, it was a mark of social standing in the community to be in church. It was a mark of higher social standing to be in a mainline Protestant church.

During the post-war period children of school age were in "the family pew" with their parents. It was a sign of growing up when they were old enough to join the youths who sat together in the back row or in the balcony. For the most part, children and youth were present for congregational worship as a matter of course. However, even those who did not worship regularly did attend Sunday School. Parents who were not active church members felt constrained to make sure that the children went to Sunday School anyway. Sunday School and Church were the Protestant Sunday ritual. No one asked why. As long as Sunday Schools and youth groups were meeting regularly or grow-ing—as long as churches were involved in building programs—clergy and laity were hopeful and optimistic about the future of the church.

In the public schools there were rarely objections to daily Bible reading and prayer or to the Protestant form of high school baccalaureate services. The local priest may have been asked to participate, but he was not invited to plan the service. In predominantly Protestant towns and villages, going to the Catholic church was second best, but better than no religion at all. In areas with a predominantly Jewish population, Protestant youths resented their own minority status in the public schools. For that part of the population still "unchurched" there was Billy Graham, who worked carefully with local church federations in an effort to channel new converts into a "church home."

For that same post-war generation, it was assumed that church-going would continue when youths went to college.

University chapels overflowed on Sunday mornings. College students worshiped at local churches, and some provided leadership for those congregations. For those who attended college, getting married and finding work was the next step. Failure to achieve either objective seemed somehow abnormal. High school graduates who did not go to college or trade school were expected to find work and to marry.

A mother knew she was a success if her children followed the prescribed pattern. Her crowning achievement was visible whenever the family was together again—at worship in "the family pew." Though parents might have been unhappy knowing that some of the younger generation were there under duress, it did not matter a great deal. The important thing was that they were there. Young adults, now parents, had the baby baptized, possibly to please their mothers. Sometimes the baby was baptized in the home church of the maternal grandmother rather than in the church where the parents were members. The mother who insisted that her children and grandchildren maintain traditional religious rituals was faithfully living out the role assigned to her in the vision of "a Christian America."

The Peter Marshall sermon, "Keepers of the Springs," is a classic example of the dominantly Protestant Victorian family ideal. Marshall uncritically accepted the roles assigned to men and women in the American Dream as the nation returned to "normal" patterns of work and family life. He sacralized this set of cultural ideals by proclaiming the roles to be God-given. The sermon was intended to instruct young women on their role, lest women forget their proper sphere of influence. During the war, women played an important role in the workplace by filling positions vacated by men who went to war. But the entrance of women into the workplace was acceptable only because of a national emergency. A return to normality required "women who will lead us back to an . . . old fashioned decency . . . to old fashioned purity and sweetness for the sake of the next generation."[12]

In another sermon, Marshall noted that if a woman tries to assume equality with men, she automatically steps down "from the pedestal on which Christianity, chivalry, and idealism has placed her." That step will cost her her "moral standards," "ideals," and "essential femininity." Her proper work, which Marshall implies is really more important than the work of men, asks of her *only* that she give "her full time to her home, her husband, her children."

According to Marshall, men cannot carry out their work in the world unless they have a good woman waiting for them at home. She should try to

> understand her husband's work . . . to curb his egotism while, at the same time . . . encouraging all his hopes to establish around the family a circle of true friends. . . . If she can do all this she will be engaged in a life work that will demand every ounce of her strength, every bit of her patience, every talent God has given her, the utmost sacrifice of her love. . . . It will demand everything she has and more. And she will find that for which she has been created. She will know that she is carrying out the plan of God. She will be a partner of the Sovereign Ruler of the universe.[13]

Peter Marshall identified the roles of Christian men and women in carrying out the plan of God with the needs of the nation. "America needs young women who will build true homes." He seemed to believe that unless a man had a wife faithful to her domestic calling, he could not meet the demands of the world on him in his workplace. This theme, identical in every detail, is typical of scores of sermons and bride-books written by men for women after the Civil War.

Marshall assumed that woman's sphere was a God-given role necessary to the well-being of family and nation. In this vision of "a Christian America" the church serves as a source of moral inspiration that will ensure national morality, power, and success by maintaining the stability of families. From his perspective, the woman's sphere was as essential to the well-being of the nation as the contribution of man. For the "springs" being kept by American women were the source of character and moral integrity of future citizens.

Peter Marshall's sermons demonstrate the way in which pastors uncritically foster cultural ideals by giving them divine status as God's will. Visions of "a Christian America" had unusual power to shape and inform the values and attitudes of children and youth growing up in the period in which Marshall was a well-known public figure. The American victory in World War II revived a belief in American morality that had been associated with America as a world power since the end of the Civil War. An obvious, continuous rise in the standard of living after the Civil War was widely perceived as God's special blessing on a moral nation where slavery had finally been eradicated. By the end of the nineteenth century the connection of national prosperity with national morality was so common that union leaders, politicians, and pastors all talked of "Christianizing the world in our lifetime."

The dualistic ideals associated with the Victorian family and the national dream of "a Christian America" gave Americans a way of life based on family loyalty and hard work. The separate-but-equal approach to the private work world of women and the public work world of men was taken for granted for about 130 years, from 1830 until approximately 1960. Throughout that period a stable, intact family unit was considered essential to national prosperity and to moral progress.

The American family was believed to be the building block of the nation, the very foundation of all Christian civilization. Any change in roles assigned to men and women was seen as a threat to family stability, to the future of the American Dream, and to the future of God's whole creation.

## Family, Church, and Culture in Transition

"The Christian Family Church is often haunted by the Golden Era which glows a little with increased distance and immediate difficulties."[14] That golden glow is usually associated with a return to "normal" life after World War II. Men came home; families were reunited; there was a baby boom. An unusually high proportion of Americans were church members. It was a time when the American people renewed their faith in the God who gave them victory in war. During the 1950s the basic elements of the American dream were recovered with compelling force—family stability, a rising standard of living, and seemingly unlimited career opportunities.

Any Protestant who came of age in some small town in post-war America experienced a kind of cultural homogeneity that no longer exists. They learned the same moral code—the values of a Protestant America—at home, at church, and at school. Although not everyone kept the code, it was clear that church members were expected to conform.

Although honesty, hard work, and thrift were encouraged, it was attitudes related to sexuality, marriage, and family life that were most explicitly conveyed. The moral code included prohibitions against masturbation, premarital intercourse, extramarital intercourse, and homosexuality. Young adults were encouraged to marry only within their own religious and ethnic group. Interracial marriages were not discussed. Divorce was possible but rare. Marriage was assumed to be lifelong. Certain misfortunes that might befall a family were not discussed in public—a child born out of wedlock, adultery, suicide. It was a misfortune if a young adult remained single, or a couple, childless.

The freedom movements of the 1960s posed a direct challenge to the American way of life so clearly articulated during the 1950s. The loyalties of generations of church-going Americans were called into question as the civil rights movement became an anti-war movement and then a war on poverty. The limits of freedom were tested as demonstrators took to the streets and to the barricades on behalf of an array of freedoms—race, religion, sex, age, and conscience.

Nothing less than a cultural transition was under way, with protests led by the disenfranchised: the young, the Afro-American, the poor, the aged. Some protests were led by women, an unprecedented development in American history. Everyone had a dream. Like a rainbow, the dream had many hues. But each hue was still recognizable as that of the American Dream. Everyone wanted the dream to come true for them.

Even as the meaning and limits of democratic freedom were being tested, technological achievements that would change the living and working patterns of all Americans occurred. The instantaneous flow of information through the telecommunications industry altered personal communication and human relationships. The presence of television was changing relationships at home, at work, and at church. The ability of nations to communicate within minutes of the occurrence of an event altered the way people experienced time and history.

But it was medical technology that most immediately affected daily life, that challenged all traditional definitions of morality and personal ethics. For the first time in American history inexpensive, reliable birth-control methods became available to the public. Radical changes in sexual self-expression accompanied an unprecedented freedom from fear of conception. The response of pastors and theologians to these issues has been sporadic. Denominational attempts to give moral guidance through policy statements are usually met with apprehension and theological conflict.

It is unmistakably clear that there is no longer a standard form for a family. The average life-span has increased from 60-65 in 1900 to 70-75 in 1985. A marriage now has the potential of lasting longer than ever before in history. Better health and longer lives mean that people have more productive work years than ever before. The abilities to control the process of procreation and to delay death raise fundamental issues about life and death in a new way.

The 1980 census report indicated that nearly one-half of people ever married are divorced. The number of people staying single doubled between 1970 and 1980. Compared to the ideal American family of "the family pew," 23 percent of all households in 1980 consisted of one person living alone. One out of every five children lived with one parent—a 33 percent increase since 1970. A new study indicates that 57 percent of Catholics under 30 have never married; 41 percent of Protestants under 30 have never married.

Church-going parents of single young adults cannot expect their children to accept the moral code learned by their generation before the sexual revolution. No moral issue has the kind of black-and-white clarity for people born after 1960 that it had for those who came of age before 1960. Americans born after 1960 are not imbued with the family ideals of the American Dream. Christian parents wonder how to respond to all the issues that are now part of daily family life. They can no longer assume that values taught in public schools are those taught at home or at church. They often get little help from the church in thinking through the many issues that divide the two generations—those born before and those born after 1960.

The reemergence of a Victorian family ideal as part of the vision of a Christian America in the 1950s was an epiphenomenon, a temporary spark of life in a dying ethos. Had the resurgence of "the family pew" ethos not occurred, events of the 1960s would have been less shocking to church-going Americans. Since the end of the First World War, American culture had been acquiring a more urbane international flavor that did not mix well with the sexual prohibitions of the Victorian moral code. The sexual revolution of the 1960s only made obvious the changes in American sexual behavior that began after the First World War.

Protestant churches have exerted relatively little influence over moral behavior in American since the end of the First World War. Compared to the influence of church leaders through the public press and platform at the end of the nineteenth century, the church has steadily lost ground as worthy of coverage as "news" by public media. "The Church" as a social institution has had only a marginal and indirect influence on American culture in the twentieth century.[15]

After the Second World War, pastors like Peter Marshall continued to inculcate a Victorian code and the family ideals associated with it; but the life of men and women in the 1950s bore little resemblance to the lives of Victorian men and women for whom the complementarity of the sexes was a part of daily life experience. Young men and women gave lip service to ideals of moral purity being taught at home, church, and school. Yet, research demonstrated that premarital sexual activity was already more the norm than the exception.

The Kinsey reports of 1948 and 1953 were shocking only because they confirmed what careful social observers already knew—the Victorian social code had been the moral code of the

American middle-class in word only since the end of the First World War. In *Catcher in the Rye,* Holden Caulfield, that tireless cataloguer of "phonies" in the adult world, became the hero of American youth in the late 1950s because he told the truth as they knew it. Adults in his world were not reliable; his life experience contradicted the ideal of that happy American family he had only heard about.

The so-called sexual revolution of the 1960s was not a sudden explosion of oversexed youth. Nor was the seemingly sudden disintegration of family life a sign of the end of the family. Both events signaled the end of the power of a Victorian sexual ethos to inspire Protestants to live according to the values of "the family pew."

What appeared to be a sudden change in national moral values was not discontinuous with developments in American culture since the beginning of the twentieth century. The Victorian moral code that was taught and sustained in Protestant churches had become unworkable in the culture at large. The great surge of patriotic spirit and church-going after World War II was accompanied by a revival of a Victorian family ideal. Yet, it was that decade of renewed family idealism and uncritical patriotism that was discontinuous with twentieth-century cultural history. Against that one decade of apparent calm and normal "apple-pie" life in America, the freedom movements and demonstrations of the 1960s appeared to be an aberration. They were, in fact, only a phase in a longer cultural transition in which the stated ideals and moral codes of the Victorian era were gradually being discarded.

*Responses to Change in "The Family Pew"*

The typical congregation at worship on Sunday morning no longer looks like "the family pew" of the post-war period. Congregations are greying. There are fewer children at worship with their parents. If children are at worship, they often leave the service after the children's sermon. Unless there is a youth choir, the population of the back pew may be sparse. College students and young adults are even less visible. Statistical reports are not needed to verify what is obvious: The power of "the family pew" has declined. There are more older adults in the church-going population but there are also fewer younger families in most churches. As church membership has decreased, so has the relative percentage of active members, Sunday School enrollment, and optimism about the future of the church.

Concern about the future of the church is most obvious in relation to children and youths. Quite literally, these groups are the future. Responses to change or perceived decline in the church are usually attempts to restore the sense of well-being associated with "the family pew" after the Second World War. As change in the family has become obvious, several strategies have been tried to attract younger families.

Churches in the more conservative Protestant traditions attract new members and are growing because they still support "the American way of life." To participate in the life of a conservative congregation is to experience life as it seemed to be in the post-war period. The life of a Christian is described according to the moral standards and social roles associated with "the family pew" ethos; few members would object to the way a woman's role is described in "Keepers of the Springs." Members of conservative congregations are self-consciously conserving the values of the American Dream. They are confident that America will return to a Christian way of life if the moral standards of the past can be reclaimed.

Liberal congregations are more likely to adapt teaching and traditions to the tempo of the times. More liberal churches experiment with groups for singles to meet new needs. They are more likely to change worship traditions to appeal to modern people. Members of such churches may prefer a dialogue, children's sermons, or clown ministry to the traditional sermon. They may prefer the ambiance and intimacy of informal worship to the stuffy boredom of more traditional liturgy.

Liberal congregations have a new tradition—a shorter, less formal family service designed to include children in worship. Some of the new forms of worship and much of the "family service" is little more than worship at a child's level of comprehension, not unlike the opening exercises of the Sunday School. This is the liberal way to recover the well-being associated with "the family pew"; it preserves the appearance of the tradition without trying to teach an obviously dysfunctional moral code.

Congregational response to change in the family usually takes one of two forms, strategies to preserve the past or strategies to adapt to the present. Both have the same objective; most congregations want to see their buildings bustling with activity and growing as they did after the Second World War. Leaders of congregations continue to hope for a future when "the family pew" will look the way it did then.

## Domestic Captivity in Protestant Congregations

Before change in sexual behavior and family structure challenged the moral commitments of "the family pew," anthropologist W. Lloyd Warner had observed that beliefs and practices in the church and in the family were so intertwined that, "Should the present form of the family disappear, the Christian church would necessarily undergo revolutionary changes."[16] As he studied the values of American culture just after the Second World War, Warner concluded that the symbol system giving moral form to life relationships—especially family relationships—was a sacred symbol system. In his study of the way Americans order and interpret their lives through rituals and moral codes, he found that religion and family were dependent on each other in supporting a symbol that gave meaning to life and moral behavior.

The extensive use of family language and metaphors found in most Protestant ritual represents the kind of symbiotic union between the church and the family that Warner considered dangerous. A symbiotic, or dependent, relationship in the natural order is a relationship in which two organisms live in a close and mutually advantageous union. However, the union can become unbalanced to the point that one organism saps the life and vitality of the other.

Warner's observation that the Christian church would necessarily experience revolutionary change "should the present form of the family disappear" was prophetic. The form of the family in American culture has been unstable and changing since the early 1960s. Protestant old-line congregations have experienced loss of members, purpose, and direction ever since.[17]

When the life experience associated with religious language changes, the rituals of a religion lose their power to give meaning to the lives of believers. The extensive use of family language in Protestant liturgies today no longer connects with life experience as it did when it emerged in the cultural experience of a Victorian America.[18]

It is striking that a major change in the form and function of American families does coincide with considerable reorganization in Protestant denominations. The mission and purpose of Protestant congregations was related to their reputation for undergirding the morals of the nation by supporting the family unit. In reality, Protestant influence has been a less vital force in shaping twentieth-century American values than many church leaders have imagined.

*Religious familism* refers to the use of religious language and rituals to express and reinforce family commitments. There is a kind of *folk religion* or *domestic religion* in which believers use God as a means to achieve their own ends. Where religion has become domestic the rituals of a particular religious tradition are identified with seeking God's blessing for the family-related hopes and desires of believers. Beliefs of the religious tradition are adjusted accordingly.[19]

A folk religion is always related to, but different from the historic faith from which it springs. Religious familism is the American folk religion; it adapts the language, symbols, and rituals of the Christian tradition to serve the family needs of the people. Ideals from the Christian tradition are conflated with those of the American democracy to express the hope for "a Christian America." Americans tend to uncritically identify loyalty to family with loyalty to church. Congregations in which loyalty to church and family are virtually synonymous are engaged in an American form of religious familism.[20]

As evidence, consider the results of recent research concerning the importance to laity of various tasks performed by pastors. Preaching, pastoral care, and administration are at the top of the list. Laity say that they would not be likely to consult with their pastors about an ethical or a work-related issue. Of all the tasks of the pastor, leadership in mission and leadership in evangelism are of least importance to both pastors and laity.[21] Preaching, pastoral care, and administration are valued primarily for personal reasons. The symbiotic union between church and family has become unbalanced to the point that family-related needs have become a major preoccupation of congregations that have turned in on themselves.

The captivity of Protestant congregations in visions of a domesticated church leads to a severely truncated vision of the nature and mission of the church. It threatens to reduce the role of a pastor to that of family chaplain. Clarification of the legitimate roles of both pastor and people in the congregation depends on being able to distinguish the role of the church from the role of the family in the lives of Christians. Chapter 2 is about the way "the family pew" ethos affects program planning and leadership roles in congregations.

# CHAPTER 2

# "The Family Pew" and the Church Today

For most of American history a belief that America is a Christian nation has sustained the ideals of the American Dream. Since fulfillment of the dream depends on a nation of moral citizens, the role of churches has been associated with the support of family life. Since the early 1960s American culture has become increasingly secular in outlook. Just as schools are no longer dominated by a Protestant ethos, American morality is no longer dominated by standards considered Christian. There are few broadly shared standards for ethical behavior in American culture today.

Although no new national myth has emerged in place of the long-standing belief that America is "God's new Israel,"[1] it is clear that American culture is a secular culture. Even though American people are very religious, that does not mean the culture is devoted to serving the God of the historic Hebrew and Christian traditions. The broken connection between Christian religion and American culture leaves Protestant churches in the ambiguous position of being conservers of the values of a Victorian worldview.

Role confusion is a classic sign of cultural transition. As early as 1960, sociologists of religion reported that pastors and laity experienced congregations as fragmented.[2] That was only the beginning of the larger cultural transition that has continued ever since. By 1970 there was evidence of role confusion among pastors and laity. Both groups reported feeling unclear about their respective roles in the church. Continuing redefinition of ministry and ordination procedures indicates that role confusion in the church has not yet been resolved.

During the 1960s change in sexual behavior and family roles led some social theorists to predict the end of the family. In retrospect such responses seem overly dramatic. But they are evidence of the extent to which an intact family, performing "God-given" roles at home and in the world, is essential to belief in the American Dream. Articles in church periodicals and nonreligious news magazines alike predicted a dark future for America as the divorce rate began to climb. The prediction of the end of the family as a social institution was wrong. Changing moral standards, and changing roles for men and women do not mean that the family has come to an end. It does mean that most Americans no longer believe in a Victorian family ideal.

Church leaders typically respond to major cultural transitions about twenty to thirty years after social institutions begin to change. The churches of America are culture-conserving institutions. Even the most liberal denominations like the Unitarian Universalists function to conserve the cultural commitments of the middle-class status-quo. Despite the equality acquired by women and AfroAmericans during the 1960s, members of middle-class churches are still relatively unaware of the extent to which most congregations are still sexist and racist. Victorian dualisms continue to be operative in a congregation if members separate church life from daily life.[3] It is dualistic to believe that American culture is secular but church members are sacred, as if they do not live in "the world." It is dualistic to perpetuate roles and traditions that subordinate women to the authority and wisdom of men, either in the church or in the family.

The continuing power of Victorian ideals is evident in the fact that after twenty years of ordaining women to ministry very few women have been appointed or called to become head-of-staff in a larger congregation. The very term *head-of-staff* has masculine connotations, just as *Christian educator* almost always means a woman. It is dualistic to perpetuate a division of program responsibility between a lay-led Sunday School staff and a pastor-led church program.

## The Impact of Victorian Dualisms on Protestant Pastors

Confusion in the church today about ordained and non-ordained leaders is related to a lack of clarity about the role of the family and the role of the church in faith formation. The historic Protestant expectation that the pastor has primary responsibility for interpreting Scripture to the people through preaching and teaching changed in the nineteenth century. Responsibility for teaching about the Bible and Christian tradition began to shift to two other locations—"the Christian home" and the Sunday School.

According to the script of the American Dream, the family was essential to the hope for "a Christian America." Since parents were expected to nurture citizens according to a Christian standard of moral behavior, church leaders assumed that children would learn Christian attitudes from their parents at home. Parents were also expected to teach their children about the Bible and Christianity. The Sunday School was started to provide Christian nurture and knowledge of the Bible for poor children who lacked the advantages of middle-class family life. In this sense the home and the Sunday School were both expected to be "a little church" in which children and young people could learn the moral values of Christian citizens.

The Christian home has not functioned as a center for family Bible study for well over a century among most church members. Yet a persistent myth about the family as a little church reappears whenever the future of the family in America seems doubtful. In such times Protestant church leaders double their efforts to encourage parents to play their "God-given" roles in making sure that their children will be Christians.

Attempts of pastors to encourage parents to have family devotions does little more than induce guilt. Membership patterns in most denominations encourage adults to join a church without any serious preparation for living a Christian way of life. Many do not even know about, let alone practice, a disciplined life of faith—daily Bible reading, meditation, and prayer. Adults who lack knowledge of Scripture and prayer can hardly be expected to communicate faith to children at home.

Since 1960, new curriculum intended to reinforce Sunday School lessons by asking parents to teach their children at home, has been introduced by several main-line denominations. The outcome is inevitably disappointing. The fallacy in this approach is exposed in the following observation.

> One of the sacred cows of the evangelical subculture is the family altar. In our thinking it has stood as the norm for a healthy Christian family. . . . Central to the problem of the family altar has been the unexamined acceptance of it in theory, while the non-practicing silent majority listen with respect, feeling a bit guilty at this hiatus in the family life.[4]

The evangelical subculture is not alone in uncritical acceptance of family-related sacred cows. Recent Episcopalian attempts to develop a curriculum that would engage parents in the "catechesis" of children at home also failed. This is only a new word for the long-standing Protestant commitment to the idea that the Christian family should be a little church. Only in a tradition where adults continue to refer to the family life of individual church members as "the Christian home" would pastors, educators, and theologians have continued to believe for so long that parents are more important than the church is to the faith of children.

The idea that parents can or should worship with children at home assumes that church members who become parents are committed, self-disciplined Christians who model Christian behavior at home. Continuing fruitless attempts to make the family an agency of the church assumes that church-related parents are spiritually mature Christians.

The weak link in this chain of sterile admonitions to nurture children at home comes from the Victorian belief that children learned to be Christian first at their mother's breast. The significance of mother-love and piety on the faith commitments of their children was overrated by Victorians. Continuing belief that the children of a Christian mother will automatically be Christians accounts for some of the unrealistic expectations about the family in the church today. The importance of "the Christian home" in the religious socialization of children has been so taken for granted that until quite recently the formative power of the congregation has been neglected.

## The Family as a Means of Grace

Salvation in the Catholic tradition depends on having access to the means of God's grace primarily through the church. Traditionally, the priest has been more important than Protestant clergy as mediator of grace through the sacraments. During the nineteenth century, the spiritual power attributed to parents—especially mothers—gradually undermined the priestly role of the Protestant pastor as an agent of God's grace. Ever since, there has been less importance attached to regular participation in worship and the Lord's Supper among Protestants. The power attributed to parents in the faith formation of their own children means that the Protestant family was expected to function as a means of grace in the lives of family members.[5]

The way church programs are organized reveals the operative understanding of the church about the role of the pastor. Most Protestant pastors in Victorian America believed in the sanctifying power of the Christian home. Faith in the nurturing power of the Christian home was shared by both liberal theologians like Horace Bushnell and conservative evangelists like Dwight L. Moody. Moody would not have disagreed with Bushnell's belief that "a child should grow up not ever having known himself (sic) to be anything other than Christian."[6] Bushnell believed that if a young child was influenced for good early enough in "a Christian home," a conversion experience during the impressionable teen years would not be necessary. The only real difference between a Bushnell and a Moody concerned whether children must also have a conversion experience in order to know that they are Christian.

These assumptions about the faith formation of children in "a Christian home" are a deeply embedded legacy from the Victorian period.

> To understand the Christianity of this period [Victorian] we must look not only at public symbols of civil religion . . . but at the sacramental character of the home. Domestic Christianity provided Protestants and Catholics with a sense of stability in a climate of social and religious change. For Protestants the ideology and symbols of the home served as an alternative to sectarian splintering by presenting an agreed-upon notion of an eternal, God-given, Bible-based family life.[7]

Implicit belief in the power of a good woman as a moral influence in the lives of children and men continues wherever Christian nurture in a good home is believed essential to the process of becoming Christian. The expectation that a mother or a motherly Sunday School teacher could teach the Bible to children gradually eroded Protestant concern with careful interpretation of Scripture. This practice implies that any Christian can understand and teach the Bible. It raises the question as to why a pastor is needed.

### Dualistic Attitudes About the Roles of Men and Women

The belief that one can grow up never having any identity other than that of being a Christian depends on the unbiblical assumption that children are born innocent and that human nature is maleable—a clean-slate theory of moral development. It assumes that a child will become like the most influential persons and ideas experienced early in life. If a child has positive moral influences and Christian nurture from birth, Christian identity will imperceptibly take shape over the years. Christian faith, from this point of view, is as natural as biological development. Given a good mother and a positive environment, any child should flourish; or, lacking Christian nurture at home, a positive Sunday School experience may do.

Horace Bushnell was typical of almost all Victorian social theorists and pastors.[8] They described human nature in dualistic terms by misconstruing the meaning of the New Testament concerning "spirit and flesh." They constructed a doctrine of sin out of a New Testament observation that sometimes "the flesh lusts against the spirit." From this they concluded that since the lower "animal" nature tempts the "higher" spiritual capacity of human beings, most sin is sexual in nature. To them the higher nature or "spirit" meant mind and conscience, the faculties of reason.

They reasoned that if the mind is filled with good ideas—like Bible stories and tales of moral virtue—most people will act accordingly. That is why Bushnell considered the early influence of parents at home so terribly important. Parents provide not just attitudes about life but the earliest content of the mind as well. There was the possibility that the "flesh" could lead a good person astray at any time of life, if "animalistic" urges overpowered the "spirit." But temptations of "the flesh," especially among men, was the great source of sin. The steady influence and love of a good woman was the countervailing influence most likely to keep Christian men from corruption by unmanageable sexual desire.

Any Victorian would have readily agreed with the philo-sophical injunction that the virtuous person will put "reason in the driver's seat," lest the conscience be overwhelmed by some sudden outburst of passion. They assumed that people or groups appearing to them to be less intelligent—and thus less reasonable—had a limited capacity for sexual self-restraint. By definition, homosexuals were unreasonable and animalistic. Black people were more like animal "flesh" than human "spirit," even if not responsible for that situation. Homosexuals and black men were expected to commit crimes of a sexual nature.

The emergence of leaders like George Washington Carver gave hope that some "negroes" were educable. In both cases, civil rights could be—and were—denied to homosexuals and black persons because they failed to meet the culture's definition of human "spirit," meaning a reasonable and sexually self-controlled person.

Although white women were considered the moral superiors of men, they were denied civil rights on other grounds. From the perspective of the family ideal, women already played a crucial though indirect role in the public arena as wives and mothers. Their husbands could speak for them in public life. Belief in the pivotal role of the family in American culture made it difficult for many in the church to see any need to support suffrage for women. It seemed unnecessary.

These views on human nature and sin were stated explicitly in most religious literature during the Victorian period (1830–1913). Although their language would sound quaint today, a dualistic view of human nature torn by the lure of the flesh against the spirit has simply gone underground. It is still the basis of judgments made in American culture about who is and who is not an acceptable and reasonable person. This view of human nature lies behind attitudes considered "racist" and "sexist" today. The courts still assume that a reasonable person would not commit a crime; that is why a "crime of passion" can be attributed to temporary insanity!

In her study of Protestant and Catholic attitudes about "the Christian home" between 1840 and 1900, Colleen McDannell shows how Protestants came to rely on the mother, rather than the father, as the priest in the home. This division of labor in the home is reflected in a similar way of thinking about church programs and in attitudes about church leaders.

> Protestants maintained the virtue of home worship but slowly moved the father out of his position as the household priest while moving mother into her role as family minister and redeemer. Moral instruction—a teaching ritual—came to replace worship as the primary goal of Protestant family devotions. This instruction was child-centered, mother-directed, and individual. While paternal authority continued to be acknowledged and male involvement desirable, fathers were increasingly edged out of a Protestantism which stressed innocence, personal piety, individual education, and the sanctity of domestic sentiments.[9]

Until pastors become aware of the ways in which the dualisms of the Victorian family ethos have been institutionalized in the church, confusion about their own role as spiritual leaders in a congregation will continue. Victorian attitudes about male and female roles are perpetuated by the division of labor between the Sunday School and church.

These attitudes still affect the way pastors feel about tasks they associate with Christian education. Many pastors, male and female alike, have an aversion to any association with the Sunday School. Like the father in the Victorian family, the pastor was edged out of a role in educational ministry in the congregation. The outcome is a dualistic attitude about preaching and teaching. Ordination is associated with preaching and a primarily masculine authority in the pulpit, while the domestic or feminine task of teaching is associated with laity who teach—Sunday School teachers and nonordained Christian educators.

The dualism of separate but equal roles associated with men and women in ministry is perpetuated in denominations where pastors are ordained, but Christian educators are consecrated. This is a clear indication that the spiritual power and authority of Christian educators—usually women—is subordinate to the spiritual power and authority of pastors—usually men. The separation of Christian nurture and teaching from the role of the pastor has greatly diminished the importance of the teaching office of ordained ministry.

According to Victorian ideals the family table was fully as important as the Lord's Table to faith formation. It was certainly more accessible. When mothers were expected to teach the Bible to children at home, they were more important than a pastor in forming the spirit of a child. The power attributed to Christian nurture at home implied that the Bible is the book, not of the church, but of the Christian home. That is one of the reasons that the Bible has been a best seller in America.

Although most of these attitudes are unfamiliar to mothers in the church today, they remain the presupposition of educational ministries in most congregations. A modern mother would not think of herself as the priest of the family. Change in family living patterns makes it difficult for a family to gather daily for a common meal, let alone set aside time for family devotions. Nevertheless there is still more concern about the dwindling importance of the family meal than evidence of desire among Protestants to gather more often at the Table of the Lord.

Although life in most families has changed radically since 1960, family-pew attitudes appropriate to life in the nineteenth century are still associated with the meanings of *Sunday School* and *Church.*

### "Sunday School and Church": A Structural Dualism

The Religious Education Association was founded during the early decades of the twentieth century. The Christian educator as a church "professional" who is distinguished from an ordained pastor is a fairly recent phenomenon. The founding of the R.E.A. represents formal acknowledgment that the teaching task associated with women in the home had moved into the church in the role of the Sunday School teacher. The teaching role of women gained professional status when churches began to hire paid professionals to supervise all Christian education. This approach to faith formation in the church still presupposes that love is learned in "the Christian home." That is why pastors and Christian educators rarely see that the quality of relationships in the life of a congregation is a part of Christian nurture.

The programmatic structure in most congregations still reflects Victorian assumptions about the role of Christian parents in the faith formation of children. Movements in the church to restore the Sunday School to the formative role it once played in the life of a congregation should be evaluated in terms of where members are expected to acquire Christian attitudes about life. If a desire to reenergize the Sunday School still presupposes that Christian nurture occurs in the home, Bible study in the Sunday School, and worship in the church, this will perpetuate long-standing misconceptions about "the Christian home."

In practice, there is often competition between the role of the pastor and worship-related church programs and that of the Sunday School in faith formation. Each part of this double program structure claims to be necessary to the faith formation of members, while ignoring the role of the other. Most congregations have "Sunday School people" and "Church people" who rarely meet, even in worship. When Sunday School and worship are held at the same time, this tells members that either learning about Christian faith or the importance of worship and the sacraments to Christians is optional. The competitive nature of this programmatic dualism is most obvious where a separate building to house the Sunday School—the Christian education unit—stands side by side with the sanctuary.

People who participate in the "opening exercises" of the Sunday School learn an ethos. Their identity as Christians is influenced by that ethos. The Sunday School was once a major religious institution in its own right, with its own staff, its own budget, and its own worship. This is still true in many congregations, but on a smaller scale.

The Sunday School was once the evangelistic wing of many congregations, recruiting new families through Sunday School children. That is why church leaders who want to bring back the past imagine that church membership decline can be reversed by rebuilding the strength of the Sunday School. The Sunday School had, and still has, a worship tradition with its own music. There may be a Sunday School songbook different from the hymnal used in worship. Sunday School songs are more evangelistic: they often stress personal piety.

Pastors sometimes feel as if they are competing with a "Sunday School theology" in their attempt to lead a congregation. That hunch is correct. There is a difference in the spirituality, the beliefs, and the language used in the worship of the Sunday School and that of the church. A pastor who ignores the Sunday School runs the risk of letting the Sunday School form the faith commitments of members. This is most likely in small-town and rural congregations where allegiance to the Sunday School is still more powerful.

Opening exercises in the Sunday School have no sacramental element. This exercise in folk religion may include a homily or object lesson presented by a lay leader. The suspicion of some pastors that this ritual represents laity "playing church" is not entirely unfounded. The fact that opening exercises are usually didactic and instructional in nature can influence attitudes about worship in the sanctuary. That may be one of the reasons that so many adults like the children's sermon in worship. They may be more comfortable with moralistic teaching about what a child *should* do than they are with proclamation about what God is doing.

Practices associated with a Sunday School theology represent continuing uncritical allegiance to the ethos of "the family pew." It is the way laity express their belief that the children of church members are born into the church. The implicit reason for most recent innovations in "Sunday School and Church" programs is the same—to insure that the children of members will join the church.

The Victorian belief that children who are born to church members will automatically grow up to be Christians has not changed. Instead, expectations about the nature and responsibility of church membership have been adjusted. This is especially obvious in current confusion over the purpose of confirmation classes. This minimal period of instruction about church membership is often the last formal learning experience of church members. An adjusted expectation reflects the desire of parents and pastors to keep children and youth in the congregation long enough to confirm their baptism.

Innovations in infant baptism may also inadvertently encourage belief that anyone born into a church family is a Christian. Some pastors now introduce a newly baptized infant as a new member of the family of God, a brother or sister in Christ. To the theologically untutored this may convey the idea that the act of baptism makes a Christian, or that baptism is essential to salvation. This identifies baptism with church membership in a way that diminishes traditional Protestant reliance on growth in faith through lifelong access to Word and sacrament in corporate worship.

If this description is accurate, then—in practice—the sacrament of infant baptism may be identified with salvation in a way similar to Roman Catholic theology before Vatican II. If coupled with less emphasis on preparation for confirmation, the Protestant practice of infant baptism may seem essential to the salvation of infants and children in congregations where few members ever open a Bible.

The theological justification for infant baptism depends on the commitment of parents and members of congregations to the task of rearing the children and youth of the church "in the nurture and admonition of the Lord." However, if church membership is not experienced by adults as a way of living in the world that depends on faith in Jesus Christ, infant baptism may only foster spiritual complacency and reliance on an empty ritual.

The inclusion of baptized children of church members in the Lord's Supper may be a genuflection to continuing illusions about the efficacy of "the family pew."[10] The practice of infant baptism and the inclusion of children in the Supper implies a belief that the faith of parents is more important than the congregation to the faith of children. Telling parents that they must now decide when their children are ready to participate in the Supper is like telling them to conduct worship at home. It presupposes that parents are persons of deep faith capable of conveying the importance of the Supper to their children.

These innovations related to the sacraments reflect an implicit theology in which the element most crucial to living the Christian life is missing—the attitude of faith in Jesus Christ that is essential if teens and adults are to appropriate the grace promised to them in their baptism. The church does give access to God's love and grace through baptism to all *who repent and believe in Jesus Christ.* The reception of God's grace through baptism does not automatically confer new life on the recipient; participation in the Lord's Supper does not necessarily change the recipient of bread and wine.

Christian faith is not inherited; each generation, each individual, must learn faith anew.[11] Recent Protestant innovations in membership procedures and sacramental practices are only the logical extension of long-dysfunctional assumptions about the faith formation of persons in the home, in Sunday School, and in the church.

Protestant membership rituals have always included baptism

and a profession of faith. The form of the ritual and expectations of participants vary widely. Today, most Protestant denominations require members to be baptized and to profess faith in Jesus Christ as Lord. The acknowledgment that Jesus Christ is Lord can be a life-changing event. All too often a profession of faith is no more than a perfunctory membership ritual identified only with attending confirmation classes. It follows that the incorporation of new members who have already been baptized and confirmed into a congregation will require little more than attendance at a new-member class in which loyalty to the congregation is cultivated.

If infant baptism, the confirmation of baptismal vows, and new member rituals do not require a potential "member" to know, do, or be anything in particular, no one should be surprised that congregations lack spiritual vitality. If these rituals require no clear commitment to regular worship, disciplined study, and participation in ministry by members, then there is little reason to expect church members to be different from the members of any other voluntary organization.

Family worship services and family ministries are attempts to cope with a cultural transition that threatens the viability of the present organizational structure of most congregations. It is obvious that "Sunday School and Church" are not what they once were. Yet, to add "family ministry" as another category in a long list of educational ministries is a mistake. Unless there is a new approach to the role of churches in relation to the family life of members, programs designed for "Christian families" will only reinforce unrealistic expectations about "the Christian home."

Christian faith has been domesticated wherever family loyalty and love dominates the commitments of members. It seems fair to say that there are members in every congregation for whom family commitments are the strongest motivating force in their religious beliefs and practices. If family loyalty controls the events that matter most in the life of a congregation, the faith commitments of that congregation are misplaced. If love of family is stronger and deeper than love for Jesus Christ, this is family idolatry.

# CHAPTER 3

# The Effect of Family Idolatry on a Congregation

W here a domesticated piety dominates the commitments of a denomination, the conservation of middle-class ideals can blind both leaders and people to the prominent concern for social justice found in the Bible. On the other hand, even when leaders are committed to seeking social justice, they have not been able to sustain a legitimate critique of poverty and injustice in America because the family ideals of the American Dream continue to be linked to democratic values and economic stability. Uncritical loyalty to "the family pew" makes it very difficult to see or comprehend the plight of the poor and the homeless, the oppression of minority persons, as anything but their own fault. It requires courage for any pastor of an old-line congregation to preach prophetically. To ask middle-class Americans to see American culture as Jesus would see it is to ask them to vote against their own privileged position in society.[1]

## Dualism in the Nature and Mission of the Church

The United Presbyterian Church was seriously divided in 1971 over a $10,000 contribution by the Council on Church and Race to a legal defense fund for Angela Davis, a black activist and revolutionary. While the division of opinion revolved around whether the church should ever get involved in politics and whether Christians could support a known communist, the unspoken issue was the historic suspicion that communism is an attack on the American way of life. Among denominations in which membership was already declining in that period, the United Presbyterians experienced the sharpest decline in stewardship as well.

Because of deep division over the "Angela Davis affair," Dean Hoge conducted a survey among United Presbyterians in New Jersey to learn why the action of the council had drawn such extreme reactions. Hoge's conclusions are not surprising when seen in the context of the role of churches in perpetuating the American Dream. His data, published in 1976, convinced him that American Protestants are divided into a two-party system. The major difference between parties concerns the relative importance of outreach and mission activities in a congregation. He found that liberals define mission as support of social action and oppose evangelism; conservatives define mission as evangelism and oppose social action.

More important, Hoge discovered that mission and out-reach—regardless of definition—is not the ultimate loyalty of either party. Liberals and conservatives agreed that serving the needs of members and their *families* is more important than outreach in either form. The "needs of families" are identified with career and standard of living. "If a proposed action is perceived as contrary to middle-class interests, even some persons who favor 'social action' in theory will begin to oppose that particular action."[2] The value consensus of conservative and liberal Protestants is the middle-class way of life. For both, commitment to religion and church is seen as a way to fulfill personal goals related to family, career, and standard of living.

Hoge's data is not peculiar to Presbyterians. The data indicates the general controlling power of family loyalty, possibly the most powerful remaining loyalty in the vision of "a Christian America." Church members seem determined to maintain the belief that their church is a family of families. Even if members do not view the family as a little church, they still want the congregation to be a family of families.

Present confirmation practices affirm the belief of parents that their children have been born into the church and should be confirmed. However different private and public visions of the church may be, they do agree on maintaining the status of "the family pew," through worship, Sunday School, and pastoral care.

The two spheres of the dichotomous worldview of Victorian America are reflected in these attitudes about the nature of the church. The private-party church is devoted to saving individual souls, one by one—to drawing the world into the church for spiritual safety. Just as the Victorian home was considered "a haven from a heartless world" the evangelical church offers safety from a dangerous, immoral world to its members. The pastor takes on the role of the mother—instructing, nurturing, inspiring, comforting members in times of trouble. Like the Victorian mother, the pastor presides over family worship.

The "Christian family church" is usually a private-party church: concern with personal morality is high. Members want the pastor to take a stand on moral issues as long as the position taken claims to be biblical and conforms to their moral values and commitments.[3]

For the public-party church, the nature and mission of the church require some form of activism in the world, the public sphere of Victorian men. The pastor's role here is more like that of the Victorian father, with far less emphasis on instruction or nurture of members. Pastoral care may be secondary to the work of inspiring members to find some ministry in the community. Worship, preaching, and the sacraments are rituals of congregational identity for world-oriented people. The modern social gospel is a masculine, worldly form of Christianity. Here, too, members want the pastor to address moral issues only as long as the position conforms to their moral and political convictions.

Either way, the pastor is expected to model the gospel that is preached. Congregations look for a pastor who models their form of Christianity while serving as in-house family chaplain for members. The pastor is expected to lead the congregation by strengthening its particular identity. Effectiveness is generally measured by how well the pastor conforms to local expectations, adds new members to the roll and money to the treasury. Members of most congregations would not want their pastor to give spiritual direction to their congregation if that meant a challenge to present commitments.

The "family pew ethos" institutionalized in late-Victorian Protestant spirituality depended on an unquestioned belief that Christian faith is most powerfully nurtured in the Christian home, while knowledge about the Bible is best learned at church. Unless pastors acknowledge the truth that the church cannot rely on the home for nurturing Christians, congregations are doomed to keep repeating the dichotomous patterns of a Victorian worldview.

The belief that love and moral commitment are learned at home while persons learn about the Bible at church has had the devastating effect of separating life at work and life at home from the life of faith. That is why there is so little transfer of learning from the church to daily life in the world. The Protestant churches have institutionalized a split between church life and the daily life of church members for so long that members either do not want or do not expect their pastors to relate the Bible to their loves and moral commitments.

It is doubtful that Protestant families ever functioned as little churches. But it is certain that unless that illusion is named and confronted, the present gap between church life and the daily life of church members will not be bridged.

*Confronting Family Idolatry*

The loyalty of church members to visions of an ideal family is a tragically misplaced love. Where love of parents, children, or spouse commands more commitment than love to God, the one who loves is bound to be disappointed. Love to family members and spouse can be an expression of love to God. But that is different from the kind of faith *in the family* found in many congregations.

The 1961 survey of Fairchild and Wynn reported an "unhealthy ultimacy" in an expectation of "complete self-fulfillment" in family life among parents of children attending Presbyterian Sunday Schools. They also found that the parents interviewed knew very little about Christian faith. This suggests that the attitudes about the family held by most adult church members are not very different from those of any other American.[4] One difference is that members of congregations expect the church to help them achieve fulfillment in their family relationships.

There is little reason to believe that parental expectations of the church have changed much since 1961. The idea that a family can be a source of self-fulfillment has a tenacious hold among the ideals that Americans hold dear. Even if this ideal is no longer as important to Americans in general, research indicates that the life of many congregations revolves around their reputation for being "a family church."[5]

Love of family is still a dominant loyalty in Protestant congregations. Jesus was quite clear that anyone who loved family more than they loved him would not be found among his followers (Matt. 10:34-39). This suggests that attempts to keep the loyalties of "the family pew" intact in a congregation is a tragically misplaced loyalty.

American Christians are so imbued with a subtle mixture of love of country, family, and God that it is difficult to see this as a false god. It is hard to condemn love of family or patriotism. Nevertheless, Protestants in America have been dreaming of a Christian America for two hundred years; they have known only a Christianity in which God has been identified with prosperity and family stability. The hope that God will bestow blessings on family members seems more like a form of Old Testament tribal religion than the post-Pentecost faith of Christians who "turned the world upside down."

Jesus commended the scribe who saw that to love God and neighbor above all else "is much more important than all burnt offerings and sacrifices" (Mark 12:33). The scribe recognized that preoccupation with religious traditions—even those commanded by God—can become idolatrous. When any act of faithfulness becomes so important that the activity obscures the ability of the people to know and praise the faithfulness of God to them, then they have forgotten that God is the source of all human love. "The family pew" is an American form of the ancient Hebrew tendency toward preoccupation with burnt offerings.

Whenever the people of Israel became preoccupied with religious ritual they lost their capacity to enjoy God's love for them. Any love more important than God's love can become an idolatrous love. Amos's condemnation of an idolatrous form of religion is as clear today as it was at the height of Israel's power and prosperity.

> I hate, I despise your festivals, and I take no delight in your solemn assemblies. Even though you offer me your burnt offerings and grain offerings, I will not accept them; and the offerings of well-being of your fatted animals I will not look upon. Take away from me the noise of your songs; I will not listen to the melody of your harps. But let justice roll down like waters, and righteousness like an everflowing stream. (Amos 5:21-24)

## Membership Growth and Decline

It is striking that congregations once considered main-line have become "side-line" since the freedom-movement era of the 1960s. No subject has commanded as much attention among pastors and denominational leaders in recent years as that of declining membership in formerly main-line churches. The Church Growth Movement offers books, workshops, and evangelism programs to stem the tide of membership loss.

Leaders say that spiritual vitality of members is as important as the number of members. Yet, maintaining some level of financial viability does get priority over spiritual formation when membership is declining. Freedom of religion means that a free market forces pastors, congregations, and denominations to compete against one another for members. Ecumenical cooperation can only flourish when churches are growing and financially stable.

Like the economy, American congregations have regular

periods of growth followed by precipitous decline. During the past twenty years sociologists have tried to explain why some denominations and congregations grow while others lose members. It has been argued that conservative congregations are growing because there are clear expectations concerning what a person must be and do in order to become a member. Where there is clarity about what a congregation stands for, members do have more conviction about their faith.

In congregations that are not growing there is often lack of clarity about group identity. Over time, a diminishing sense of commitment to the church affects the morale of the congregation. Members are not likely to give the church high priority in their lives if belonging requires no particular effort on their part. People cannot be expected to invest themselves in an organization that asks nothing of them; if little is required that is exactly what they will give.

Research about adults who are "church shopping" indicates that they want to find a congregation with good worship and preaching, a church where the people are "friendly." But they are also thinking about the person most likely to be with them in times of family transitions. They want a pastor with whom they will feel comfortable at a family baptism, confirmation, wedding, funeral. Denominational identity is less important to most church shoppers than finding a pastor and congregation where they feel comfortable. In part, it is family-pew loyalties that lead people across denominational lines. They are looking for a church that will satisfy the needs of their family members.

Loyalty to "the family pew"—and to "our kind of people"—is a powerful motivation that directly affects church membership choices. It also has an effect on denominational policies concerning sacramental practices, definitions of membership, ministry, and the role of pastors. Trends toward increasing homogeneity in the membership of congregations are troubling indicators of lack of concern about racism, sexism, and classism in the church.

Sociologists have studied, probed, and measured change in church membership patterns over the last twenty years, trying to understand the precipitous decline in membership. The prognosis is not all gloom and doom. The latest phenomenon among the now "old-line" churches is the growth rate of churches with 1,500 or more members; this accounts for virtually all membership gains in once "main-line" denominations. Otherwise, small "old-line" congregations grow smaller. The average size of most congregations is now 100-150 members on the roll.[6]

Most of the growing churches with 1,500 or more members are located in the South and Midwest. These are the two regions where the conventional values of "the family pew" are still strong. Just as economic prosperity and church-going habits have always reinforced each other as family-pew values, the towns and cities in which churches are growing are usually located in regions where there is recent economic and population growth.

In recent years the Southern Baptist Convention, one of the most explicitly conservative denominations, has grown. Denominational leaders are quite explicit about preserving the values of "the Christian home" and the moral standards associated with the God of "a Christian America."

A combination of economic growth with the conservation of the dualistic worldview of Victorian America—especially attitudes related to sexuality—partially accounts for growth in conservative churches. At the June 1988 Southern Baptist Convention, delegates voted unanimously to condemn homosexuality as "a manifestation of depraved nature" and "a perversion of divine standards.'"[7] There is some evidence that when church-shoppers look for a church with lively worship and good preaching this includes a concern for moral values they can affirm.[8]

In the northeast, where church membership losses are greatest, there is far less economic expansion. The moral standards of a "new" sexual ethos dominate urban centers and influence attitudes of church members in the northeast. The spirituality of the sexually conservative family-pew ethos is far less attractive to persons living in the northeast than it is to persons living in the south and midwest. Nevertheless, wherever churches are growing it is often because they remain faithful to some of the attitudes and aspirations of the American Dream.

Sociologists report that strong Sunday School programs attract couples with children to a particular church. Studies of growing multiple-staff congregations indicate that the two most important factors that attract new members are good preaching and worship and "a friendly congregation."[9] These are also the churches most likely to have a well-organized Sunday School with classes for all ages.

The emotional climate of any congregation with more than 1,000 members has the appearance of warmth but makes no particular demands of members. It has friendly looking people who exchange casual greetings or do church business before and after worship. It is very likely a church where each age group and interest group has its own proper place. The capacity to offer more than one time for worship and Sunday School usually means that children will attend their classes while adults worship. That way adults can enjoy quality sermons and a good choir without being disturbed.

In a large congregation only a small percentage of adults will ever be asked to participate actively as leaders of the congregation. A growing congregation bustles with life; the staff is excited and exciting. Morale in growing congregations is almost guaranteed to be high. Yet, here is a "church home" where anonymity is also guaranteed to anyone who wants it. Where there are more than 1,000 people who worship on a given Sunday morning, intimacy can easily be avoided. The membership rituals in a large church, of necessity, can be little more than a perfunctory introduction of persons who will never know or be known to more than a small group within the congregation, if they are known at all.

The personality of the pastor is crucial to a large, growing congregation in a way that is not true for smaller congregations.

There is [also] evidence that the pastor's influence on church membership growth increases with the size of the church. Many members in mid-size churches and most members of large membership churches listed the pastor along with the friendliness of the people as the principle reasons for joining their present church. In churches with fewer than 100 members, the pastor may or may not be a critical factor in church membership trends.[10]

The pastor is less likely to be a critical factor in membership trends in churches of one hundred or fewer members because of the natural capacity of the small congregation to be like an extended family. Here, there is usually a stable core of members who provide ministry to family members in times of need. Whether the pastor is a critical factor in membership trends or not, people are looking for a "church home" where they can expect someone to be with them in their times of family transition or crisis.

Membership in all but a handful of congregations today is relatively casual, making few demands of persons who indicate interest in a congregation. Current statistics indicate that the larger the congregation the faster it will grow. The rate of growth, percentage of membership at worship, health of church finances, and percentage of budget given to benevolence are typical measures of a church's success.

This all too typical quantitative measure of church success is like the standard of success in the Victorian family where wealth was considered evidence of God's blessing on good people. For a long time the wealthiest people were thought to be the best, most moral people. No main-line denomination ever condemned the "ill-gotten gains" of any "captain of industry." Denominations and pastors were only too happy to benefit from the philanthropic impulses of the rich.

None of the above factors—membership growth, financial stability, a friendly congregation, quality worship, or good preaching—is necessarily evidence that members are committed to participation in the Body of Christ. Where gains in church membership do represent commitment to participation in the Body of Christ, the surrounding community is aware of a Christian presence in its midst. Often a congregation is known because of its ministry to various kinds of family situations. Where members of a congregation are expected to embody the Spirit of Jesus, their attitudes about family life, work, and stewardship are distinctive. Their commitments of time and self to seeking well-being for others in the congregation and in the world can attract new members.

Members of congregations that lack clear identity often treat the church as a peripheral activity. If the membership standards of a congregation do not indicate the all-encompassing nature of faith in Jesus Christ, it is likely that membership commitments will be perfunctory.

*Exclusive and Inclusive Membership Practices*

Most conservative congregations have clearly stated expectations about what their members stand for. Some require their members to have a particular kind of religious experience as evidence of the work of God in their lives. It may be a conversion experience, a spirit baptism, or speaking in tongues. There is still an expectation in many conservative congregations that members should worship regularly, study the Bible, and support the congregation financially.

Liberal theologians who favor "inclusive" membership policies tend to believe that a congregation will exclude people who are different if there are stated principles regarding church membership. They are rightly suspicious if the principles are the sexist and racist values of the American Dream. But they are wrong if they also conclude that a congregation should not have any requirements of its members lest this lead to a spiritual elitism.

An inclusive church, by sociological definition, is one where no one is excluded from membership because he or she lacks some distinctive mark of calling such as a conversion experience.[11] This way of distinguishing exclusive from inclusive membership policies misses the point that all children born into a religious tradition will be encouraged to conform to the practices of their parents. For instance, among so-called exclusive Baptists where a conversion experience is required to become a church member, young people can be expected to have a conversion experience. But among inclusive Presbyterians where membership may have been considered a family tradition, youths are expected to confirm their baptism. Any religious ritual can come to seem like a requirement for membership when it is the tradition.

Old-line denominations are almost always inclusive in their membership practices. They distinguish themselves from their more charismatic or pentecostal brethren by the very fact that they do not exclude anyone from their membership by spiritual distinctions. They function more like the civil religion of the state churches of Europe, insofar as members are usually born into the church. That is, most members think of themselves as "birthright" Christians. Membership in an inclusive church is often associated with family and citizenship. The implicit old-line mark of a work of God is birth into a white middle-class Protestant family. Here, too, children are expected to conform to the religious practices of their parents.

Is it only a coincidence that old-line denominations have declined in the same period when middle-class parents find themselves less able to expect their children to conform to the family tradition? A recent analysis shows a 30 percent decline in Presbyterian church membership from 1965 to 1988 despite a 27 percent gain in the United States population in the same period. Jack Marcum points out that if the membership loss is attributed to a declining birth rate the decline should have started in the early 1950s. "A more plausible explanation of membership decline among Presbyterians—at least in the beginning—is in terms of the denomination's declining ability to hold onto those [members] who have been reared in Presbyterian families."[12]

Whether the membership policy in a congregation is inclusive or exclusive, both have been deeply influenced by "the family pew" tradition of the American Dream. Either way, most new members come into fellowship because they are either children of members or friends of members. People who are not like member families socially will not feel welcome. Either way, there are distinctions that are often, though not always, indicative of class affiliation. A visitor to any congregation will know if he or she is in the "right" place by simply observing the dress, the manners, and the language used by members.

It is not exclusive membership requirements that make people feel they do not belong in a congregation. It is the attitudes and values that are acted out by the people who are members which make people feel excluded. This exclusion is a reality for homosexual Christians who are not able to be themselves in many congregations. Although no statistical data are available to verify that homosexual Christians are members and pastors in many congregations, the statistical probabilities from other national data would suggest that concomitant numbers of pastors and laity are homosexual in orientation; however, most do not reveal their identity as homosexuals. They may choose to conceal their identity rather than risk becoming objects of fear and prejudice of other members.

Studies about church growth indicate that a major factor in growth is a homogeneous congregation.[13] The most homogeneous congregations in America today are those that are committed to the values of "the family pew." However, the price of uncritical commitment to "the family pew" is the perpetuation of attitudes that will make anyone who is the "wrong" color, class, or sexual orientation feel excluded. Under the surface of many successful congregations catering to the needs of middle-class families lurk the stereotypes and prejudices now ruled unacceptable in civil law. It could be concluded that laws intended to guarantee equal opportunity to all persons are more Christian in intent than the attitudes found in many congregations.

Membership in a church "family" can become idolatrous if a congregation includes only people who are socially comfortable with one another. If people who are "different" feel uncomfortable then that congregation has a membership policy that is exclusive in practice if not in theory. Present practices give an outsider the impression that church members and their pastors are right while the outsider must somehow be wrong. As in Jesus' day, this may be a case of members of a religious tradition imagining themselves acceptable to God only because they are not like the "sinners" and "outcasts."[14]

### Spiritual Direction as Prophetic Ministry

It may seem like a contradiction in terms to suggest that giving spiritual direction to a congregation is a form of prophetic ministry.[15] Yet, many Protestant congregations are in a state of spiritual drift, in bondage to some part of the American Dream. Although denominational leaders, seminary professors, and pastors may know that dreams of American manifest destiny influenced nineteenth-century theology, few seem to recognize the ways in which the American Dream still influences the church today. The task of giving spiritual direction to a congregation that does embody some of the attitudes of a family-pew theology calls for pastors with the convictions of a prophet, able to tell the people of God that their loyalties are misplaced.

Times of spiritual drift can occur when the present theological tradition is no longer adequate to the task of describing the meaning of Christian faith when there is a major cultural transition. This is one of those times. Recovery of spiritual vitality comes through leaders who feel compelled to speak the word of God to the people. Whether that impulse comes through the preaching of a George Whitefield, the spiritual search of a Martin Luther, the passion for justice of a Sojourner Truth or Martin Luther King, or the humility of a Pope John XXIII, renewal always comes from a rediscovery of the spiritual power of the gospel. Spiritual renewal today depends on awakening to the power of the gospel to transform persons through the Church.

There are signs of new life in the church today. Spiritually restless Christians join Bible study groups, prayer groups, healing groups. Some are church members; some are not. Some of the most impressive evangelism and justice ministry is being carried out by ecumenical groups outside of denominational affiliation and power structures.

Those who write denominational policy continue to respond to role confusion among pastors and laity by redefining *ministry*. Laity are now better represented at every level of corporate decision-making than ever before. But this stab at inclusiveness and equality in ministry bears virtually no relationship to what happens in the life of congregations. It indicates that political power to make decisions has been confused with spiritual power. A quota system will not lead to spiritual renewal. Neither will a redistribution of the responsibility of ordained leaders of the church among the laity.

Pastors—not the mothers of America—are "keepers of springs" of living water. But their responsibility for Word and sacrament will be surrounded with ambiguity unless they are able to claim the ministry to which they were ordained. In the midst of confusion about the ministry of all Christians it may seem reactionary to claim that the role of a pastor is to give spiritual direction to a congregation. Protestants do not think about ministry in terms of spiritual direction. Yet, the writer of Ephesians indicates that it is the life work of church leaders to "equip the saints for the work of ministry . . . until all of us come to the unity of the faith and of the knowledge of the Son of God, to maturity, to the measure of the full stature of Christ" (Eph. 4:12-13).

Leaders of congregations should be people who have been set aside to care for the spirit of other Christians because of their own spiritual gifts and sensitivity. God calls such people to serve as teachers, preachers, evangelists, and prophets to strengthen the unity of the church through knowledge of the Son of God. How else might pastors equip laity for their rightful ministry if not through offering spiritual direction for their lives?

The spiritual authority of a pastor depends on a capacity to interpret Scripture so that it becomes good news to the people of God. It depends on ability to plan and lead worship in which God's love—a love too great to be conveyed by words alone—is experienced. The provision of spiritual direction for the life of a congregation requires the courage of a prophet to challenge illusions about "the good life" and the gentle love of a shepherd who leads a flock to springs of living water.

The office of ordained ministry has traditionally been defined as responsibility for Word, order, and sacrament. The church in the late twentieth century is no different from the church in any age in her need for leaders to feed God's people by telling them the truth about God, the world, and themselves. To ask a pastor to give spiritual direction to a congregation is another way of saying that the church needs leaders who can help people come to know that God loves them through their study of Scripture, participation in the sacraments, and membership in a fellowship of Christians.

It is rare to find a congregation where members realize that it is the life work of all Christians to seek and find God's will, that this is learned through corporate Bible study and prayer. In recent years, the Protestant tradition has not cultivated the practice of traditional spiritual disciplines among either pastors or laity. Yet, these are the disciplines that undergird, inspire, and sustain the commitment to Christian ministry. They are the disciplines that give direction and meaning to life.

Ordination to ministry sets people aside to be responsible for the care of the human spirit through Word and sacrament. Extensive involvement in pastoral care leaves some pastors spiritually depleted. Where the pastor is the only person making calls in times of family tragedy, the only person sought for counsel in times of trouble, this can lead to a misuse of God-given gifts for ministry.

This does not mean that ministry does not require sensitivity to the particular needs and circumstances of members of a congregation. It does mean that more pastoral care should be carried out by members of a congregation so the pastor can devote more attention to the disciplined study and meditation necessary for lively preaching of the gospel, teaching, and worship leadership.

In practice, most senior pastors enjoy this luxury. They are known for their gifts in preaching and worship leadership. If a congregation is to know the power of God's word, the pastoral leader needs time to learn what it means to faithfully exegete Scripture. Every pastor should be able to devote at least one full uninterrupted day a week to Bible study and sermon preparation.

A pastor is not called merely to provide spiritual services for a congregation. If any one person gives excessive amounts of service, other members are robbed of growth through ministry. Every Christian has some gift for ministry, some way to give God's love to others. The exercise of gifts for ministry is essential to growth in commitment to Jesus Christ. The task of the pastoral leader is not to do all of the work of the church; it is to engage all of the people in all of the work of the church. That is what it means to give order to the life of a congregation.

Very few Protestant pastors ordained in the last thirty years have been educated to think of themselves as the spiritual leaders of a congregation. A theological education may represent little more than learning about theology, the Bible, and church history; it may seem unrelated to being a spiritually disciplined person. Yet, the very same knowledge can be spiritually formative if it is expected to inform and transform the life of the learner.

Just as theological studies can impact the life of the learner, a pastor's preparation for preaching, teaching, and leading worship each week can be spiritually formative. These preparations are the practices of a spiritually disciplined person. It is through preparation to lead others into fellowship with God that a pastor acquires the spiritual vitality that is communicated through acts of preaching, teaching, and leading worship. Any pastor who leads a congregation so that members can see God's grace at work in their lives and in their world is already giving spiritual direction to that congregation.

The next step—leading others into ministry—depends on the pastor's understanding of the nature of ministry. The focus on ministry as spiritual direction requires the pastor to become the servant of all, the person who enables the ministry of every other member of the congregation. To accomplish this objective would require a redistribution of work in most congregations. In that process, both pastor and congregation will find that their understanding of the nature and mission of the church is changing.

Jesus did not begin ministry until he had been baptized and empowered by the Holy Spirit (Luke 3:21-23). The apostles could not begin their ministry until the Holy Spirit appeared in their midst on Pentecost (Acts 2:1-12). Faithful ministry in every age has been ministry guided by God's word as it is known through scripture and illuminated by the Holy Spirit. The fire of Pentecost represents the power of God's presence, the same fire encountered by Abram, Moses, and Elijah.

In the tongues "as of fire" seen at Pentecost, God made the

power of the Spirit available to every follower of Jesus Christ so that each one would be able to speak about "God's deeds of power" (Acts 2:11). The power of the Holy Spirit is promised to every pastor in ordination. Like the grace of God and the love of the Lord Jesus Christ, the fellowship of the Holy Spirit must be claimed to be fully enjoyed. That is the only purpose of spiritual discipline: that all might know the love of God.

•   •   •   •

Part 2 is a discussion of what it would mean to understand the church, the Christian life, and the family in a more holistic way. The discussion presupposes that the church cannot discuss sexual ethics in a way that is guided by dialogue with Scripture unless the dualistic views of "the family pew" are discarded. A holistic vision of the Christian life means that healthy sexuality is integral to spiritual well-being.

Part 3 is a description of the kind of church program that encourages members to embrace a holistic spirituality. In congregations where laity are engaged in their God-given ministries, expectations about the nature of the church and the role of the pastor do change. When this happens the congregation can give genuine support to members in carrying out their family responsibilities.

# PART TWO

# A Biblical Perspective on Family, Church, and Christian Life

# CHAPTER 4

# A Biblical Critique of Family Idolatry

*A*t the end of the nineteenth century many Protestants believed that American had been chosen by God to transform the whole world into the kingdom of God on earth. Even if their theology about the future of the world differed, they were likely to agree that America was God's chosen nation. The myth of America as "God's new Israel" was a part of the national self-image quite apart from formal theological considerations or specific biblical references. The values of the nation seemed Christian to church leaders who talked of "Christianizing the world in our lifetime."

This vision of the mission and destiny of Protestant Christianity in America was shared by liberals and conservatives. It was congenial to progressive politics at the time. Many church leaders believed that the dream of saving the world through democracy was simply a political way of expressing the mission of the church.

Of all the Western races, that can read skillfully the providence of God, or can read it at all, can hesitate in affirming that the signs of divine decree point to this land of ours which is gathering to itself the races which must take the lead in the final conflicts of

Christianity for possession of the world? Ours is the elect nation for the age to come. We are the chosen people.[1]

Austin Phelps, a congregational executive for missions, could speak these words in 1881, confident that his reference to God's providence would motivate people to increase their support for home missions. The vision of "the elect nation" is a way of interpreting God's act in history that came to America with settlers from England. In seventeenth-century England, Protestants believed that the Reformation was being worked out in England, that England was heir to the promises of Israel.[2]

The habit of associating biblical concepts like the Providence of God and the election of Israel with a nation and Protestant Christianity has greatly influenced the way American Protestants regard the nations of the world, the church, their families, and themselves. The expectation that God was bringing the Reformation to completion in America has been part of the national self-image since the seventeenth century when English Puritans settled New England and Scottish Presbyterians settled in the middle colonies.

The idea of private property as essential to a Christian civilization was also part of the English interpretation of God's Providence.[3] In the nineteenth-century American version of "salvation history," property ownership was regarded as a sign of God's blessing, failure to own property as either punishment or a sign of moral failure.

The theme of God's judgment, talk of heaven and hell, and an expectation that the end of history is imminent is far more prominent in American religion than it is in the Bible. There is no one biblical eschatology, though there are several highly symbolic accounts of how God will bring history to a close in "the end times." These symbols are commonly employed to call the people of God's chosen nation back to faithfulness.

Many of the ideas associated with the American Dream are no longer expressed in nineteenth-century terms. Yet, the association of God's blessing with prosperity continues to have formative power in American life. Low morale in congregations experiencing membership loss and financial difficulty has deeply rooted spiritual dimensions related to the American Dream. When a sanctuary is half empty it can feel like a divine judgment.

Protestant response to changing family roles has a similar spiritual dimension. Many Protestants still measure the success of their family according to the ideals of the American Dream. When children do not share the values and attitudes of parents about sexuality, marriage, or family, parents feel they have failed. This, too, can feel like a punishment from God.

### A Biblical Perspective on Church and Family

The use of Judeo-Christian symbols and values to express the American Dream continues to influence the way Protestants use and understand the Bible. The use of biblical language to express a Victorian worldview makes it very difficult for most Protestants to remember that the books of the Bible address questions posed in another time in terms of the worldviews of ancient cultures. The nineteenth-century sense of certainty about a hierarchy of moral, social, and intellectual values remains a part of the way many in the church today still regard family ideals.

Historian William McLoughlin describes the thought of Horace Bushnell as typical of nineteenth-century "Romantic Evangelicalism." He points out that a "romantic view of the Bible as literature or poetry proved a convenient way to rationalize much of the higher criticism."[4] According to McLoughlin, Bushnell's adaptation of Judeo-Christian symbols and values included a belief in intuitive perception of truth, a Christocentric theology and a "sentimental idealization of women, children, and parenthood as the most perfect embodiments . . . of grace."[5]

Contemporary discussions of Christian education differ little from Bushnell's way of reasoning. The family ideals of the American Dream are rarely evaluated from a biblical perspective. It is not uncommon to find Victorian dualisms read into a biblical text about the family or sexual ethics.

In books about "the Christian home" writers seldom note that the New Testament is about the faith of a religious community. If they are from a biblically conservative tradition they are likely to use selected references to sexuality, marriage, and family to communicate the ideals of God in a way that will encourage and motivate people to strive for the ideal.[6] This didactic use of the Bible fails to distinguish the radical difference between family life and the religious practices of ancient and modern cultures.

On the other hand, liberals writing about family life or sexual ethics know that "the family ideal" is not viable for Christians today. They may find the Bible an inadequate guide because they *are* aware that the books of the Bible were written in a variety of settings in ancient cultures.

As church members and pastors try to adjust their minds and hearts to the way family relationships have changed, few seem to realize that the family ethos that is changing had very little in common with a biblical perspective on the role of the family in the life of faith. The issue is not the validity of Scripture as a guide to faith in contemporary culture. Rather, the issue is the validity of a family ideal that is believed to be biblical.

Biblical scholars concerned with the roles of men and women in biblical cultures point out that the love ethic of the early church was so revolutionary in its day that it was considered a threat to social order in the Roman Empire. The loosening of kin-family loyalties in favor of church-related loyalties was perceived as dangerous. Elisabeth Schüssler Fiorenza finds the roots of patriarchy in the very earliest responses to Jesus' treatment of women as equals.[7]

The scenario she describes is not unlike the response to the changing roles of women in contemporary culture and in the churches. Many commentators see the changing role of women as a threat to social order and personal morality. Much of the resistance to change in Protestant churches today comes from people who fail to realize that a Christian way of life is far more radical than it would appear when looked at uncritically through the lens of a family ideal that has roots in the American Dream of the nineteenth century.

All interpretations of the Bible are relative to the interpreter, the interpreter's critique, and the conditions, times, and places of the text. In every period of the history of Christianity, the church has had favorite texts and favored interpretations. Nevertheless, it is possible to get a perspective on family life by asking what informs reflection about the family in the New Testament. In the following discussion, questions will also be raised about what factors might have governed the judgment of writers.

What does the New Testament have to say about family life? The Gospels tell the story of the life, death, and resurrection of Jesus in terms of his own Jewish tradition. Each Gospel writer encourages first-century Christians to remain faithful to their baptism, but in slightly different ways. The stories they tell to instruct the faithful are addressed to congregations with reference to particular circumstances. Each Gospel is written in a way that keeps the power and hope of the Risen Lord vividly alive to memory and imagination. This is the Christ experienced by Christians through the ages as the life-giving Word of God through scripture.

Most of the epistles and pastoral letters are also written to specific congregations. In the Gospels, Jesus is presented as a charismatic figure who places loyalty to God clearly above all other loyalties, including family loyalty. According to the Gospel, he had very little to say about families. The epistles and pastoral letters give more direct attention to family life in the short passages known as "a household rule." Similar passages in Colossians 3:17–4:1 and Ephesians 5:22–6:9 contain instructions to men and women, parents and children, masters and slaves. These passages have been cited a great deal as support for American family ideals and hierarchical relationships.

The "household rules" of the New Testament are included in books addressed to members of missionary churches. As such, the rules bear little relation to modern concerns such as fulfillment in family life or even the quality of family life. The biblical writer's concern about family relationships is that of an evangelist. The issues addressed are those of ways Christians can witness the love of God to non-Christians in their own families and in their communities.

In a "household rule" it is the behavior of individuals in their role as family members that concerns the writers. The reason for the concern is always that of how family relationships will affect the church. A careful reading of the rules in Ephesians gives the impression that the relationship between members of the congregation is considered the primary family of Christians. The writer expects their identity as "children of light" to inform their family life and responsibility as family members.

The writer of Ephesians thinks about the daily life of Christians in terms of service to God and to one another. The new life in Christ requires the believer to walk in love "as Christ loved us and gave himself up for us, a fragrant offering and sacrifice to God" (Eph. 5:2). In the context of a discussion about the new life in Christ, general teaching about sexual purity, wise use of time, and the pleasure of praising God in song preceded a more specific discussion of husband-wife, parent-child, and master-slave relationships.

As if to reiterate the sacrificial nature of the way in which the faithful are to "walk in love," the writer warns of the forces of evil ready to deceive Christians with illusions about the fruits of sin. The attitude of faith described is that of a quality of life, a way of relating between Christians at home that has direct continuity with the worship life of the congregation.

Parental responsibility includes the admonition to bring up children in "the discipline and instruction of the Lord" (6:4), a favorite verse in modern "Christian family life" literature. In the first century, Christian parents were probably expected to teach "the law" to children as it had been taught in the Jewish family. The continuity of early Christian communities with the Jewish tradition suggests that children would learn Christian faith through participation in worship and through home ritual. Greek assumptions about education also could have informed attitudes about parental responsibilities. However, it was the Jewish way to tell the stories of faith associated with religious rituals.

The visible mark of Christian faith, according to New Testament writers, is in the way life is lived. In both Jewish and Greek traditions, it was assumed that chastisement and correction were a part of every learning process. Just as the congregation had defined patterns of spiritual discipline intended to strengthen the commitment of the community as a group, it was assumed that all loving relations include discipline, correction, repentance, and forgiveness.

Given the theological and church issues that could have divided any one of the early Christian congregations, the importance of the Lord's Prayer as a guide to all aspects of daily life becomes apparent.

Give us this day our daily bread.

And forgive us our debts, as we also have forgiven our debtors.

And do not bring us to the time of trial, but rescue us from the evil one (Matt. 6:11-13).

This was the way of life and the ethic of disciplined love to be carried from a congregation into the nonbelieving world through believers. The social ethic for family members found in a household rule provides only general guidelines for the ordering of relationships grounded in equality in Christ. All aspects of the Christian life central to the teaching of the church—worship, ethical responsibility, deeds of mercy—were to be carried out in daily life as witness to life lived in the power of the Spirit. Wherever Christians incarnated the way of Christian love, they bore witness to the presence of the Spirit of Jesus in the world. This included life at home.

As a minority group living in a hostile culture, members of the early Christian churches were in no position to identify the bestowal of God's grace and blessing with national peace and prosperity. As a rag-tag group of believers from various ethnic backgrounds they were in no position to identify Christian faith with any one type of family.

The love ethic of Jesus had the effect of challenging the priority of all bloodline family relationships. Apparently, families were torn apart if all members did not become Christians. It was in this setting, as the church modified the sense of loyalty to family and nation of the Jewish tradition, that Christians were instructed about obligations to blood relatives.

## The Changing Role of Family in the New Testament

Among the early Christians, the church was quite literally "the household of God." That household included families, but it was by no means a collection of family units. When Christians were no longer welcome to worship in the synagogue, they moved their worship into houses and fields. The church, as the household of God, gradually modified reliance on the extended family units that had been so important to Israelite religion.

In the Jewish tradition, the blessing of God was strongly associated with a stable and prosperous family life. In the new Christian tradition, God's blessing was associated with members of a congregation. It was through the church, rather than the family, that the well-being of the new life in Christ was experienced among people who were made brothers and sisters through their common bond "in Jesus Christ."

Jesus' teaching of a "law of love" revitalized Jewish ethical instruction. Through the history of the people of Israel, two slightly different religious traditions had emerged. In the Mosaic tradition, the blessedness of the people of God was associated with keeping the covenant of law. The belief that God rewarded people for faithfulness to their religious tradition was periodically challenged by prophets like Jeremiah who reminded the people of the law of God written on the heart. In his teaching, Jesus regularly challenged legalistic religious practices, reminding his followers of the law written on the heart. He gave priority to love of God and neighbor when questioned about family, marriage, and divorce.

Parties in the church are nothing new. Just as there are parties today, writers of New Testament books had to think how to describe Christian faith to people from two different religious traditions. For Christians who had converted from Jewish religious traditions, the old forms and practices were gradually altered in light of the life, teaching, and resurrection of Jesus. Descriptions of unity in the church are usually addressed to readers with different perspectives on religious tradition.

A major theme in New Testament theology is the issue of the meaning of the church for people from these two "parties." For instance, Gentiles addressed in Ephesians are described as "converts" from the ways of the world. Compared to Jewish Christians they are seen as previously having had "no hope and without God in the world" (Eph. 2:12). Yet, the promise and hope of eternal life *in Christ* challenged prior beliefs about the meaning of life *in "the world"* for Christians with roots in the Jewish tradition.

New Testament discussions about the church are colored by expectation of the imminent return of Jesus, or the "end of the age." As the hope dimmed with the passage of time, second- and third-generation Christians became more concerned with the future of young congregations. Some scholars argue that because the churches were caught up in eschatological expectation, very little of their discussion about social ethics is relevant to modern issues.

However, scholars also point out that Gospels and epistles were written to encourage the faithfulness of adult believers in light of possible death through persecution. That is, they were concerned with the possibility of their own imminent end. They were also concerned, to some extent, about whether their children would have faith. Questions about the transmission of faith from one generation to another were surely a part of New Testament discussions about membership requirements in a Christian community. Transitions from circumcision, the traditional mark of membership, to baptism, as the new normative practice, were particularly difficult (Acts 15).[8]

The fact that Christians addressed in the New Testament came from two different religious traditions has considerable bearing on the persistent tendency to favor dualistic views of human nature and God's relationship with the world. Writers had to wrestle with the extent to which Jesus' teaching challenged traditional Jewish attitudes and practices concerning the role of men and women in the family and in Christian communities. This is most obvious in Pauline writing in which the teachings vary in different letters.

However, attitudes about proper roles for men and women were further complicated for any theologian in the early years of Christianity by differences in Gentile and Jewish attitudes about the human body. Unlike the Jewish tradition, some of the Gentile Christians addressed apparently did not consider "the flesh" essential to the human spirit. They tended to spiritualize physical reality and treated the body as inferior to and separable from the spirit.

The question of whether the biblical writers were correcting dualistic thinking or introducing it has vexed interpreters of scripture in every era of church history. The interpretation of the Epistle to the Ephesians is quite different, depending on whether the writer is seen as primarily dependent on Jewish thought and practices, or as someone whose thought is dualistic.[9] It is very difficult to know whether the writers use the various words translated into English as "flesh" and "spirit" in a spiritualizing way or not.

This, however, was not an issue in nineteenth-century American thought. No one questioned whether *flesh* and *spirit* had different connotations. The book of I Peter reads like a source-book for the dualistic theology of Victorian Protestant churches as well as new sects like the Mormons. Virtually all attitudes about sexual and family ethics are related to the belief that the passions of the flesh are the source of sin.

It is no accident that conservative Christians today are so vigilant in opposing sins they consider to be corruptions of the flesh. In their biblical heritage they are urged "to abstain from the passions of the flesh that wage war against your soul" (I Pet. 2:11). In their theology, a whole world will be lost if Americans do not return to the moral standards they take to be biblical.

### The Church as the Household of God

Contemporary Christians long for a household where they are loved and accepted as they are. There is good reason why so many pastors refer to a congregation as brothers and sisters in Christ. They are aware that many of those entrusted to their care suffer some disappointment from family members, perhaps a loss of love in marriage, that many are lonely living the single life. Given this situation, Paul's letter to the Ephesians can be especially appealing to modern readers.

The Bible can be used as a guide to faith that transcends the particularities of time and place for those who remember that both the original readers and modern readers are influenced by a culture. Parker Palmer suggests that Scripture is like a mirror we hold up to our world. In faith we judge for ourselves as a community of Christians, even if the truth we come to know is not the currently accepted "truth" of a particular congregation, denomination, or culture.[10]

Some of the continuing appeal of Ephesians lies in the use of domestic imagery and familial language with reference to the people of God. The people addressed in Ephesians were religious people who wanted to serve some God and who sought the blessings and assurances of a good life from that God or gods. They are told that the experience of being born anew into "the Kingdom of Christ and God" will raise questions about their prior attempts to be religious, good, or moral people. These were not unbelievers or irreligious people. On the contrary, they were being warned that their old way of being religious was compromising faith in the living God.

Ephesians is a letter written to warn readers against seeking more or other knowledge of God's love than is already available. Gentiles who became Christian were tempted to fall back into pagan ways of probing the mysteries of God. It is likely that they were drawn to the scientific knowledge of their time, astrology, which promised knowledge about the ultimate outcome of the cosmic battle between the forces of good and evil.

The ancient desire for spiritual power through knowledge of the mysteries of God is not unlike contemporary Christians attracted to New Age religion, belief in reincarnation, or stories about people coming back from the dead. Then, as now, the exact shape of the future was unknown. It is tempting to imagine that the forces of death and evil can be overcome by some "new" knowledge.

The writer assures the ancient readers that they need only trust the promises and knowledge of God already available to them. For they have been sealed with the promised Holy Spirit who guarantees their inheritance of life in Christ "toward redemption as God's own people, to the praise of his glory"

(Eph. 1:14). Instead of following habits from their old way of life, they are directed to look to Jesus Christ to see the kind of life that is pleasing to God. Anyone armed with the "truth that is in Jesus" will not need special knowledge because, in Christ, God's plan for the world has already been revealed.

Baptismal language is used to describe believers as persons made new by God through Christ, by "washing of water with the word." The new people of God are a people already made holy by the sacrifice of Christ. God wants the Christian community to be as beautiful as a bride on her wedding day—without spot, wrinkle, or blemish. The sins of her past are washed away. She stands on the threshold of a new life with a new family. In place of knowledge of future mysteries, the writer invites readers to participate in the present mystery of growing up "to the measure of the full stature of Christ" (4:13).

Still, life in the Spirit is described in very concrete, worldly terms. There is no indication that the power of the Spirit will lift souls up to heaven or conform believers to the moral values of their culture. This is not a theology for people who think of faith as being transferred from generation to generation. Quite the contrary, all contrasts between the "old man" and "new man," between "children of wrath" and "children of light" indicate that believers are created anew in Jesus Christ. Their prior history counts for very little compared to the transforming power of the Spirit available to the Christian community. Without the spiritual power that is given by God, they would be blind to the height, breadth, and depth of God's love for them.

*Domestic Imagery in Ephesians*

Ephesians is about the Christian community. The writer distinguishes between God as the Father to whom all believers have intimate access because of reconciliation through the cross (2:14-18) and God as the Father "from whom every family in heaven and on earth takes it name" (3:15). This suggests that the church, as the household of God, is the true "family" of Christians.

Only in Ephesians is a gathering of Christians referred to as citizens of the household of God (2:16). Markus Barth suggests that the book may be addressed to newly baptized Gentiles.[11] The household of God is meant to embody the eternal love of God which Jesus Christ graciously bestowed on all who knew him (1:5-6). The writer indicates that God's relationship to the church was established when the love of God was visible for a time in Jesus Christ.

The use of family imagery in the New Testament is the same language used to express faith in the one God of Israel. This is the God who is later perceived as the Father of all families on heaven and earth. Israel is God's "first-born Son" in the Moses stories. Salvation for Israel is sometimes conceived in parent-child language: "When Israel was a child I loved him. . . . It was I who taught Ephraim to walk" (Hos. 11:1, 3).

The association of parental language with the God of Israel was not a novelty introduced by writers of the New Testament. In the Gospels, God is said to be well-pleased with Jesus, his "beloved son" (Mark 1:11). According to the Gospels, it was highly offensive to the Hebrew way of thinking about God when Jesus addressed God as Abba, Father. It was Jesus' claim to personal relationship with the one God of Israel that was audacious to a religious tradition in which the relationship with God was a corporate experience. The father-son imagery was a new use of older, more traditional ways of thinking about the relationship of God to the world and to the people of God.

In Ephesians, family imagery is not used—as it had been in the Old Testament—to say that only Israel is beloved of God. Family imagery in Ephesians is used to express the new teaching that the beloved of God who live the new life in Christ will come from every tribe and nation. Those whose new life is assured by the love of God in Christ are bonded by a kinship of spirit stronger than the power of death and evil.

The writer reminds readers that full enjoyment of God's blessing is limited by the continuing power of evil in the world. Even so, the present oneness of God's "beloved children" in the church is a miracle among people who are bound to quarrel and misunderstand each other. The community displays immaturity and imperfection. Nevertheless, it is blessed with well-being and peace of the new life because they are united by the Spirit with Christ who loves and cherishes all of them as his own body (5:29).

*New Life and New Values*

The first three chapters of Ephesians are an exquisite description of the spiritual riches available through the blessings of God's grace. There is not the slightest hint that God's blessings are those of material reward for faithful service. There is no reference to a future reward in some mysterious place called heaven. This is a letter written to discourage airy speculations and empty words. This becomes more clear in the second half of the epistle as the writer introduces new moral and social values for Christians as the attitudes and acts of those whose "knowledge" of God comes through Jesus Christ.

The truth described is a kind of knowledge that cannot be possessed. The "truth that is in Jesus" is known as believers learn that it means to be faithful to God. The power of evil in God's world has not yet been fully vanquished. Yet, baptism into Christ places people in a family where they can begin to learn how much God loves them. The moral, social, and intellectual values of members of "the household of God" cannot be encoded in laws. Rather, the meaning of new life is grasped as believers attain "the unity of the faith and of the knowledge of the Son of God" (4:11-15).

The writer of Ephesians uses the language of courtship and marriage to convey the passion and mystery of Christ's union with the church.[12] Yet anticipation of full union with Christ does not deny the reality of inevitable daily conflict between the "old" and the "new" in the life of believers. Although the "bride" has been purified by the "bridegroom," she finds it hard to live with confidence in her new reality. Old ways of thinking about the world, the habits of the old way of life can lead her to doubt the promises of the new life in Christ.

Influences from the old life constantly affect the new life. Hence, the final warning of the writer to "put on the whole armor of God" as protection against temptation. If the community will embody the love of Jesus Christ in their relationships with each other they can withstand the power of evil in the world. There is nothing here about transforming their culture. This is warning against being conformed to the values and ethics of the powers and principalities of this world (6:10-20).

The martial language of armor, breastplates, shields, and helmets disrupts the language of love as if to convey the fierceness of the temptation to fall back into the attitudes and habits associated with the old way of life (6:6-18). Suddenly the bride of Christ is portrayed as the church militant, a people who will withstand evil in the world if they are clothed in "the whole armor of God."

Ephesians was probably not written to a particular community. It is a general treatise intended to encourage Christians to defend the good news of the gospel in the world. They are expected to proclaim the good news by living it. Family relationships are regarded as work done with "singleness of heart," rendered as to the Lord, not for the sake of impressing other people or for personal gain (6:5-10). Fidelity in the ordinary events of daily life is possible for people armed with the shield of faith, the gospel of peace, the helmet of salvation, and the sword of the Spirit.

The writer of Ephesians instructs and encourages believers regarding faithful service to each other in the Christian community and in their families. The quality of life in the household of God is a form of evangelism to a world where people are desperate for knowledge of "the truth." The "beloved children of God" are strenuously warned against falling into unfaithfulness through illusions about spiritual power offered by "empty words" and false religion.

*Freedom from Illusions About Spiritual Power*

The church of the New Testament has continuity and discontinuity with the people of God in Israel. The distinctive claim is that in the church new life is offered to all who believe that the truth about life is seen and known in God's revelation in and through Jesus Christ. That truth is so powerful that it can overcome theological disagreements in congregations. It is so powerful that it can free those who know God's love from illusions about themselves and their place in God's world.

It has been typical of the Protestant tradition to believe that "the Christian home" can or should be a little church. This reverses the biblical expectation that the power of "the love of Christ" is known through participation in "the household of God." The good life, the peace and well-being of God's blessing, is given to a community through its covenant relationship with God. God's blessing can also be experienced in the family relationships of Christians; but "the Christian home" is not the source of blessing.

God continues to create new life through Jesus Christ wherever Scripture and sacrament reveal the truth about God's intention for the world to the people of God. God creates new life through the church where the people come to know and embody the loving Spirit of the risen Lord in their love for one another. The power to move people away from their old way of life toward a new life of love of God and neighbor is bestowed by the Spirit that all might "grow up . . . into Christ" (4:15).

The essential difference between a family and the church lies in the potential for transformation through participation in "the household of God." All families socialize members to conform to the values of a particular society. In the family life of church members, parents mediate the values of the world to children even if they also express their faith in Jesus Christ in family relationships.

Membership in the household of God presupposes a common faith in Jesus as Lord. Membership in a family may presuppose little more in common than biological kinship. There is no sociological entity that can accurately be called *the Christian home*. The family is not essential to the Christian life. People can become Christian through participation in a congregation of Christians whether they were born into a Christian family or not. Only the church is essential to the Christian life.

Protestants are currently adrift in a sea of theological pluralism . . . responding inadequately to change in sexual practices and family structure. Neither the effort of the private party to conserve a Victorian ethic in the name of Christ, nor the adaptations of the public party to a cultural transition captures the essence of the gospel. As the Body of Christ in the world, each generation in the church has the potential to learn anew what it means to live in love of God and neighbor. This is the subject of the next chapter.

# CHAPTER 5

# *The Christian Life, Spirituality, and Sexuality*

*T*he quality of love experienced in a family or a congregation can be limited by the way members think about the meaning of Christian faith. Where the family is believed essential to faith, a breach of moral or social values is perceived as an offense against the family and against God. Since the nineteenth century, the sexual ethics of "the family pew" have been conceptualized in Old Testament terms without much reference to modifications introduced by Jesus' law of love. This is seen in the tendency today to think about abortion and homosexuality in terms of moral absolutes assumed to be biblical.

Many conservative Christians today have attitudes about abortion and homosexuality similar to those of ancient Israelites. In both cases, the act regarded as sinful is related to procreation. Abortion is a choice not to procreate. A homosexual couple cannot procreate.

Their attitudes are similar to the way "shalom"—spiritual wholeness and well-being—is associated with family life in the Jewish tradition. The spiritual well-being of a man depended on becoming the father of a son so that his bloodline and the religious tradition would continue in the future. Countless Old

Testament stories reveal that any status a woman had in the religious community depended on becoming a mother.

The Jewish covenant community was most defensive about religious and ethnic identity during times of exile. According to Isaiah, the "eunuch" was cast out of the Temple because he was a "dry tree" (Isa. 56:4-5). The Israelites were more likely to exclude the foreigner and the childless eunuch from their fellowship when the future of the people of God was threatened.

The teaching of Jesus that those who follow him have eternal life means that spiritual wholeness does not depend on marriage or on becoming a parent. The spiritual well-being of Christians depends on membership in the church, not membership in a family. Continuing life and the future well-being of Christians depends on fellowship with God, not generativity through procreation. Jesus' promise that eternal life is given to those who follow him does diminish the importance of the family status of all believers.

The writer of Matthew reports that Jesus shocked his disciples by commending the single life (Matt. 19:1-12). Asked about divorce, Jesus replied that if a Jewish man divorced a wife and "had" another woman, that made his first wife an adulteress. He meant that Jewish divorce laws, designed to guarantee fatherhood to Jewish men, were unfair to Jewish women. The disciples quickly concluded that "it is not expedient to marry" (Matt. 19:10). That was the point!

According to Jesus, procreation was no longer essential to spiritual well-being; he added that remaining single is not for everyone. Here, as elsewhere in Matthew's Gospel, Jesus challenged Jewish law concerning women and procreation. His point is similar to the Pauline teaching that being single is desirable because it frees Christians from the distractions of family life (I Cor. 7:32-35).[1]

According to the nineteenth chapter of Matthew, Jesus reversed Jewish belief about spiritual status. First, he granted equality to women in marriage; then he commended the status of a eunuch as having special promise for spiritual well-being (Matt. 19:12). In both cases, Jesus challenged the belief that it is necessary to marry and have children to experience God's blessing. According to him, the blessedness of salvation does not come to people by virtue of their family affiliation.

In Jesus' teaching, the last who shall be first are people who, by virtue of life circumstance, have very little social or spiritual status according to traditional religious practice—women, children, and eunuchs. He adds that the rich will have a very hard time entering the kingdom of heaven (Matt. 19:24). The first who will be last turn out to be men with social and religious status in the eyes of the world. Finally, the astonished disciples ask, "Who then can be saved?" His response was radical then; it is radical now.

> Everyone who has left houses or brothers or sisters or father or mother or children or fields, for my name's sake, will receive a hundredfold, and will inherit eternal life. But many who are first will be last, and the last will be first." (Matt. 19:29-30)

To love family members or family life more than God is exposed here as an idolatry that makes it difficult to follow the way of Jesus. This teaching raises questions about the loyalties associated with "the family pew" in Protestant churches. If Jesus gave special status in his day to persons who do not procreate, on what grounds do churches today treat modern eunuchs—single people, homosexuals, and childless couples—like outcasts?

## Theological Dualism and Sexuality

One of the contributions of biblical scholarship to the life of faith lies in the knowledge of ancient cultures now available to the church in new ways. Understanding the Hebrew perspective on human nature is crucial to any attempt to comprehend the teachings of Jesus and Pauline theology regarding sexuality. The Victorian sexual ethos relies on a misunderstanding of biblical views about human nature. The misuse of the terms *spirit* and *flesh* has been so pervasive that it is difficult for many people to think of spirituality as inclusive of sexuality in a positive way.

The extent to which sin is identified primarily with "sex" is an index of the continuing influence of Victorian interpretations of Scripture. During that period, most pastors identified the biblical term *flesh* with the "animalistic" or "lower" tendencies of persons. It was assumed that the stronger erotic impulses experienced by men could easily become compulsive and uncontrollable. Christian morality, especially for men, came to be identified with sexual purity through willed, deliberate, sexual self-control.[2]

Among nineteenth-century evangelicals, there was a conviction that God's revelation was progressive. Pastors took it as a sign of progress in their understanding of the Bible that they had come to regard sin primarily as the lusting of the flesh against the spirit. In this moral interpretation of sin, more corporate and relational interpretations of sin found in traditional Christian theology were disregarded.

Since it was claimed that God's "truth" could be known intuitively, it was possible to claim that any belief was "new light." Recognizing these assumptions about theology and epistemology helps to explain why Protestants in the United States keep repeating traditional ways of thinking about "truth." Many have amnesia about church history! As in the Victorian period, many still read Scripture as a source to reassure them that what they already "know" is "true."

When sin is defined in terms of sexual purity, the focus of the Christian life shifts away from expression of love for God and neighbor to an obsession with internal conflict between "higher" and "lower" impulses. There is less concern with evil forces in "the world" and more concern with the battle to achieve moral purity. In popular preaching and theology, spiritual power was associated with Jesus, or with the God within, who inspires and motivates Christians to overcome temptations of "the flesh," so they can do the good they know.[3]

This description of the Christian life was attractive during the early decades of the nineteenth century. It served the needs of the American democracy for self-disciplined, moral citizens. It fit well with the individual striving fostered by a fledgling capitalist economy in the early years of industrialization. Victorian use and understanding of Scripture supported a theology of the American Dream. Their misuse of Scripture is part of the folk theology of "the family pew" that still influences Protestant attitudes about sexuality and sexual ethics.

If immorality is associated primarily with sexual "sins," a dualistic psychology of "higher" and "lower" faculties is probably at work. This theological anthropology flourished in the nineteenth century partially because of the need to distinguish human beings from animals, a need created by evolutionary theories. At that time human beings were distinguished from "lower" animals by virtue of the human capacity to think and make moral choices. Hence, the association of "flesh" with the body and "spirit" with mind and will-power. When the body is implicitly associated with "lower" animal nature, it is almost impossible to think of the human body as a part of God's creation that was pronounced "good."

It is characteristic of the Hebrew tradition—and of Jesus' teaching—to think of human personality as a unity. *Flesh* can mean the body, or the skin that covers the bones. But it is also a metaphor for person, or personality. In Scripture this is expressed in many ways: Persons think with their hearts, feel with their bowels. Most important, the flesh longs for God. In Jesus' teaching the word *flesh* is used only when he quotes Hebrew Scriptures, such as "the two shall become one flesh" (Matt. 19:5). It is much more typical of his teaching to refer to human *life,* meaning life that has the possibility of being eternal.

The Pauline letters are one of the sources of confusion about *spirit* and *flesh.* However, there is little in Pauline theology to indicate dualistic thinking about human nature. He thinks in terms of the unity of personality. His analysis of personality contains a wide range of language: *soul, spirit, body, flesh, sin, reason, death, law, heart.* There is no sense in which the body is essentially sinful or separable from mind and will. The source of all sin is the knowledge that death is inevitable. Sexuality—the fact that God created male and female—is not the primal sin.

In Pauline theology, *flesh, body,* and *desire* are all used to connote sin. But desire as it is used in Scripture always means all the desires of the heart, all the loves of a person; it never means only sexual desire. Desire is necessary to Christian spirituality because it leads the restless spirit to God. But it can also lead into preoccupation with other loves, including sex.

Human nature in the biblical perspective has qualities of intelligence, freedom, responsibility. The Pauline uses of *flesh* and *spirit* to connote life orientation contrasts the quality of life lived "in the Spirit" with a life lived in bondage to the fear of death. *Flesh* and *spirit* do not usually mean that the body sins against the soul—or spirit. Paul usually means that "the law of the Spirit of life seen in Christ Jesus has set you free from the law of sin and death" (Rom. 8:2). The subject of Christian spirituality is life lived in faithfulness to the leading of the Holy Spirit.

When *flesh* and *body* are seen as holistic references to human beings it becomes obvious that many biblical references are unabashedly sexual in a positive way. For instance, to say that "two become one in marriage" is not physical or spiritual. It is both. It describes sexual union as a union of two persons just as the union of Christ with the church has visible, physical dimensions in the sacraments. The joy of the new life in Christ includes a very sensual pleasure in life that accompanies freedom from fear of sin and death. In this sense, the freedom of new life in the Spirit is almost the antithesis of the Victorian obsession with the sinful power of erotic desire. Victorian anxiety about sexual desire, the lust of the "flesh" against the "spirit," is an unhealthy preoccupation that betrays a fear of sin and death.

A biblical appreciation for sexuality, with a candid acknowledgment that sexual desire can be a force for good or evil, avoids some of the more extreme responses to the modern sexual revolution. On the one hand, there are modern libertines who claim that unbridled sexual expression causes no harm. They say that recreational sex is only play that is not significantly different from expressing other physical appetites, like eating or drinking. This perspective fails to appreciate that recreational sex can be a force destructive to the human spirit.

On the other hand, conservative anxiety about unbridled sexual appetites fails to appreciate the sheer delight of sexual union as a force for good. In general, a biblical perspective on the power of physical intimacy suggests that the sexual bond between two persons can be a force for good or evil because it is full of mystery, grace, and the fascination of the unknown.

There is an ambivalence about sexuality in some modern psychology that makes it difficult to understand the Christian attitude that sexual self-discipline can be an expression of love. If sexual self-discipline is regarded primarily as repression, then guilt and shame may be identified primarily with sexuality. Popularized versions of Freudian theory sometimes lead to a reversal of Victorian dualisms; when the values are reversed, the "worst" sin becomes denial of sexual desire! According to the biblical view of human nature, guilt and shame are related to the larger issue of alienation of the human spirit from God, self, and others.

Liberated attitudes about sex today are similar to some of the attitudes from Greek culture that found their way into the lives of early Christians. Biblically conservative Christians today rightly reject recreational sex as a psychologizing of Scripture if undisciplined sexual behavior is justified by conclusions drawn from modern theories about sexual repression. Early liberal responses to the new sexual freedom of youth had a tendency to present sexuality as the good gift of God without exploring general biblical guidelines for responsible sexual expression.[4]

Although biblically conservative Christians look to Scripture for guidance on sexual issues, most continue to read the Bible assuming a negative valuation of the term *flesh*. Their reading of biblical teachings about particular kinds of sexual activity often fails to account for the cultural setting and circumstances in which each book of the Bible was written. As a result, a biblical reference to sexuality is treated as having equal validity for Christians today. The general principle that seems to govern this reading of the Bible is the sinfulness of all sexual activity outside of marriage. Those who quote Bible verses that condemn the "sins of the flesh" are quick to point out that anyone who is immoral "will not inherit the kingdom of God" (I Cor. 6:9).

Where a dualistic approach to the Christian life is operative, people continue to associate "sins of the flesh" with animalistic behavior. For instance, people who believe that sin refers primarily to sexual perversions are likely to associate homosexuality with promiscuity.

*Homophobia* refers to an irrational fear of homosexual persons. It is also a fear of being perceived as being homosexual, especially among men.[5] The fear of being perceived as gay usually begins in elementary school when "girl," "sissy," or "fag" are the worst put-downs a boy can hear. Although the connection is subtle, the intensity of fear or hatred of homosexual persons may be linked to the fear that anyone could be overcome by their own unbridled passions. Homophobia may be the most powerful remaining legacy of nineteenth-century attitudes about sexuality.

It is characteristic of dualisms to rule out options for anyone who is different. The structure of thought associated with the moral values of "the Christian home" leads to an ethic that depends on an intolerance of variety. Why else would so many people believe that the future of "the church" depends on what the church says about homosexuality, unless they cannot imagine that there might be some options available?

## Biblical Perspectives on Sexuality

Liberals and conservatives are both influenced by dualistic habits of thought. Both reduce sexual ethics to an issue of individual choice, though for different reasons. Liberals are concerned with "rights" of individuals, while conservatives are more concerned with the "righteousness" of individuals. However, it is unusual to find concern with the way the sexual behavior of pastors and church members affects the life and morale of their congregation. Yet the effect of behavior on a community of Christians is *the* major issue for New Testament ethics.

In the New Testament, every ethical issue is a theological issue. Questions regarding sexual ethics are by definition questions about the relationship of believers with God. Body and spirit—or soul—are not separable aspects of human nature. Because the human spirit is embodied, to harm the body is to harm the spirit. Put positively, to respect the body is to respect the spirit.

From this perspective, the ordering of commitments is of great importance. Although man and woman were intended to delight in sexual union with each other, any love can become excessive or idolatrous. If the satisfaction of sexual desire becomes the primary objective in a relationship, the desire can be enslaving because it diminishes the spirit (I Cor. 6:12-20). Or, if a husband and wife live only for each other, their capacity for friendship with the community and with God will be diminished. It is not uncommon for a parent to become so obsessed with the welfare of a child that this becomes an enslaving love, harmful to the spirit of both.

People who experience intimacy with God through the church are capable of deeper relationships with friends and family. A sense of the presence, or absence, of God affects the way people relate to others, both in the church and in their families. According to this way of thinking, one of the issues for sexual ethics is how the love of two people for each other affects their relationship with God.

*Ancient Jewish Attitudes About Women and Jesus' Teaching*

Jewish legal codes varied according to circumstances of the people of Israel in different periods of their history. But laws concerning marriage generally treated a bride like property. Although there is a law recommending punishment by death to any man or woman "taken in adultery," the punishments prescribed for an adulterous woman were generally more severe than those for a man. Most prohibitions concerning adultery in Hebrew Scripture were designed to protect a man from marrying a non-virgin.

Despite patriarchal attitudes about women, family life was more important in Hebrew culture than it was to the cultures around them. Many of the laws regulating family life were designed to protect wives and children from unfair treatment. This was necessary, in part, because of polygamy. It was also necessary to ensure social stability through family harmony.

Customs and taboos incorporated in laws regulating sexuality and family life were one of the important ways the ancient Israelites distinguished themselves from other religions.

Peace and stability in family life were highly valued as signs of the special status of the nation of Israel. Because of the nature of God's covenant with Abraham, it was incumbent on every man to have heirs to inherit the blessings promised to Abraham and his off-spring. Women were valued for their child-bearing potential. Little status was attached to a woman as a person of worth in her own right. The force of this inequality is obvious in the commandment against coveting. A "wife" is listed like a slave, as a man's property. "You shall not covet your neighbor's house; you shall not covet your neighbor's wife, or male or female slave, or ox, or donkey, or anything that belongs to your neighbor" (Exod. 20:17).

Incidents in the life of Jesus provide information concerning the inequity of Jewish practices at that time. Female adultery was still punished by stoning (John 8:1-11). A man could give his wife a writ of divorce without explanation (Matt. 19:3-9). Men could be required to marry a brother's widow to insure continuation of the blood line (Luke 20:27-40). Joseph could have quietly divorced Mary when she was found "to be with child" (Matt. 1:18).

In each case the response of Jesus to these practices indicates that he sanctioned equality of treatment for men and women because God created man and woman to be one flesh (Matt. 19:5) and because God's mercy extends equally to men and women. Thus, he held that divorce is considered unchastity for a man, just as it is for a woman (Matt. 19:9). Therefore, neither a man nor a woman should divorce.

Instead of condemning the woman "taken in adultery," Jesus asked about the sins of her accusers; his point is that adultery is one sin among many. It is no more or less serious than other acts that can alienate believers from God and themselves. Jesus' nonjudgmental treatment of the woman displays the gentle mercy of the God who forgives those who repent and believe. As God is said to have "made garments of skin" for Adam and Eve (Gen. 3:21), Jesus covers the sin of the adulterous woman.

The attitudes of Jesus reveal that there is no essential difference between men and women in terms of their capacity for faithfulness or unfaithfulness to God. God loves and forgives all persons. Compared to attitudes incorporated into Jewish law, this was a departure from his own religious tradition. It was also radically different from the treatment of women in the Roman Empire. According to accounts in the Gospels, Jesus extended equal freedom and equal responsibility to men and to women.

The teaching of Jesus usually restores the intent of the Jewish legal tradition. His attitudes imply that sexual prohibitions should be obeyed, not because breaking the law will invoke the wrath of God, but because they protect the community from temptation.

Jesus treats some prohibitions even more seriously than did the scribes, but for different reasons. His concern is for the spirit of persons rather than unquestioned loyalty to the moral and social values of the religious tradition. In granting moral accountability to women, Jesus automatically called into question the way the role of women, family, and blood kin had been understood in the Jewish tradition.

## Pauline Discussions of Sexual Issues

It is instructive to Christians troubled by conflicting attitudes about sexuality in the church today to remember that the Pauline letters were addressed to congregations trying to deal with similar conflicts between cultural values. Differences in Jewish and Gentile attitudes about religious ritual, family organization, and sexual practices form the background of New Testament discussions about the sexual practices of Christians. In Paul's letter to Christians at Corinth, all discussion of sexual ethics occurs in the context of concern that Christians should not be influenced by the scandalous conduct of the pagans.

Paul warned the Corinthians against sexual immorality in the context of a discussion in which he compares the human body to a temple. As the Jewish Temple was the holy place of God, so also the body of Christians was the dwelling place of the Holy

Spirit. This refers primarily to practices of the church as the Body of Christ. When Paul elaborates the way in which all parts of the Body of Christ serve one another and are necessary to one another, it is clear that any sin that harms one believer disturbs the well-being of the congregation (I Cor. 12:12-21).

The Pauline attitude about sexuality regards sexual union as natural and good. His concern is not with genital acts as such, though his positive affirmation of sexual union is associated with procreation. As Jesus used *lust* in a broad sense to mean any excessive desire, Paul, too, describes *lust* as a darkness of mind that can lead to lasciviousness, impurity, or greed. Like the writer of Ephesians, Paul is worried about lust—burning desire—that interferes with faithfulness to God.

Individual responsibility for regulation of sexual desire is first associated with the health of the Christian community, though this also implies a concern for the individual. Since Paul considered celibacy a gift, he obviously did not expect everyone to experience sexual desire in the same way. The fact that he did not impose rules about marriage on the Corinthians—"this is a suggestion not a rule"—further implies that he was concerned for differences in individual need and circumstance. He did warn married Christians that an unnatural suppression of sexual desire in marriage could be spiritually dangerous (I Cor. 7:1-11).

The primary concern regarding individuals is that each find a relationship in which he or she could express sexual desire appropriate to their lives as Christians. This presupposes that healthy sexuality is integral to spiritual well-being. Paul's attitude means that sexuality did not have to be troublesome to Christians since they were free to choose the kind of relationship that best fit their personality. However, once they made the choice, they were expected to display faithfulness.

In the Gospels, the life and teaching of Jesus personify a law of love. The freedom of the new life in Christ, as Paul describes it, is freedom from the burden of legalistic moralisms; but it is not freedom from the ethical guidelines of the Jewish-Christian tradition. Theologians refer to the Christian ethic of love of God and neighbor as a law of love that signifies the sacrificial quality required of those who, in the name of Jesus Christ, seek the good of their neighbors. To love the neighbor is to respect the intricacies of the human spirit. The primary considerations of ethics are the effect of sexual behavior on the community and the effect of sexual intimacy on the spirituality of the partners.

## Spirituality and Homosexuality

No issue tests the ability of church members and theologians to define the nature of the Christian life quite like the question of how the church is to respond to homosexual Christians. There are at least two ways to view homosexuality.[6] Some people assume that all homosexual acts are equally sinful. For this reason they believe that the Pauline condemnation of homosexuality as "unnatural" applies to all homosexual behavior (Rom. 1:18-32).

Yet, some biblical scholars point out that this passage can only refer to the homosexual acts of heterosexual persons.[7] This is because the writers of the Bible did not distinguish between a homosexual orientation and same-gender sexual acts. If this distinction is accepted, the condemnation of homosexuality in Romans does not apply to the sexual acts of homosexual persons.

The distinction between persons of a homosexual orientation and people who choose to engage in same-gender sexual acts comes from the growing conviction that for a percentage of every population, homosexuality is a given, a life orientation that they did not choose. This is a modern idea, unknown to the ancient world.

Not only the terms, but the concepts "homosexual," and "homosexuality" were unknown in Paul's day. These terms, like "heterosexual," "heterosexuality," "bisexual," and "bisexuality," presuppose an understanding of human sexuality that was possible only with the advent of modern psychology and sociological analysis. The ancient writers . . . were operating without the vaguest idea of what we have learned to call "sexual orientation."[8]

This is very likely since the New Testament was written in a time when upper-class members of Greek culture considered a homosexual love to be a "higher" love than that of a man for a woman. As repugnant as it may seem today, the love of a man for a younger man or boy was considered especially noble. A reading of Greek philosophy of the New Testament period reveals that homosexual acts were not considered abnormal in Greek culture. These are quite likely the kind of homosexual acts described in Romans as "unnatural." These acts were subject to moral choice.

The Greeks, like the Hebrews, valued women primarily as the bearers of their children. But no man reared in the Jewish tradition would have agreed with the Greek assertion that a man could procreate with his wife, yet be in love with another man. It was precisely this kind of pagan behavior that was prohibited among Christians.

The homosexual acts considered perversions by Paul are probably references to the use of boys and young men by older men as "call boys." Pederasty was then, and still is, prohibited among Christians. But this form of homosexual behavior—an act that is chosen—is quite different from homosexual Christians today who may not remember knowing themselves as other than homosexual in orientation.

Jesus shocked his followers by granting equality to Jewish women in marriage. He commended the single life of the eunuch for its spiritual potential. Condemnation of all homosexual expressions of love in the church today can also be questioned from the perspective of Jesus' law of love. When seen as a life orientation, the issue raised for the church is no longer that of the sexual behavior of homosexual Christians. If the issue is the relationship of homosexual Christians to God, then the most important question is that of how the church can support the spiritual well-being and wholeness of homosexual people.

If it is granted that being a homosexual person is different— but not sinful—then guidelines for sexual behavior found in the New Testament apply equally to homosexual and heterosexual Christians. All Christians, regardless of sexual orientation, are offered the same privileges and the same responsibilities.

*Guidelines for Healthy Sexuality*

In the Pauline letters, sexual issues are always secondary considerations; his primary concern is the faithfulness of congregations to their calling as Christians. Discussions of sexual ethics are a response to particular situations in different congregations. There are no rules that apply to every congregation in the same way. Then, as now, it was not easy to know what freedom from the yoke of the law means for Christians.

In Paul's Letter to the Corinthians, the principle norm, or guideline, is the gospel itself. As in discussions about new life "in Christ" in Ephesians, at Corinth "belonging to Christ" means conforming life to a new identity which is given to those who confess that Jesus is Lord. "For Paul, the saving power of the cross is nothing else than Christ's love." This means that every member of a community has equal status because they are brothers and sisters for whom Christ died.[9]

In general, Paul warns the Corinthians against participation in any "idolatrous" practice that undermined their ability to be Christ's representatives in the world. This is most obvious in his discussions of religious ritual, food laws, or any form of unrighteousness that harms "the body." His point is that Christians need to be alert lest they be enslaved by anyone or anything. Hence, all things are lawful; but freedom from the repressive yoke of the law is not to be abused because "not all things are helpful" (I Cor. 6:12-13). Behavior is considered immoral or unrighteous if it works against "building up" the Body of Christ.

The issue of sexual freedom was not nearly as important in the New Testament as it is to Protestants in the church today. Sexual freedom need not interfere with love of God as the ultimate passion of Christians. Freedom from the moral values of "the family pew" does not leave the church without moral guidelines. Respect and consideration for brothers and sisters for whom Christ died are to guide the behavior of all Christians. Self-control out of consideration for others is not repression if personal sacrifice is necessary to the well-being of all members of the Body. This kind of reverence for members of "the household of God" is an expression of love to God and neighbor.

## Spiritual Formation and Sexuality

Frank Senn points out that "spirituality is not a word that has been current in Protestant vocabulary, although it is familiar to Roman Catholics and the Eastern Orthodox."

> Anglo-Saxon Protestantism is not lacking in other terms to express what is meant by "spirituality." But such terms as "godliness," "piety," "holiness of life," "the devout life," etc., have acquired unfortunate connotations. The word "spirituality" seems a clearer . . . less sentimental term by which to express the subject of communion with God and the way of life which emanates from that.[10]

*Spirituality* refers to the way people experience and express the presence of God in their lives. It refers to the way a theology is expressed through religious practices and rituals. *Christian spirituality* also refers to the way people learn to live in relation to God through participation in the church. In the Protestant tradition, Scripture and the two sacraments have been regarded as the primary means of grace through which Christ becomes a reality of life to believers. The new life in Christ has been interpreted to mean that lives can be transformed—turned around, changed, reclaimed—by the Spirit of Christ through the experience of life together in a Christian fellowship.

Recent interest in exploring the meaning of spirituality among Protestants may indicate a search for a deeper spiritual life. However, if self-fulfillment is the objective, then the new-found fascination with spirituality could be just another self-help fad. From a more traditional Protestant perspective, the sole purpose of spiritual discipline is to heighten awareness of the presence of God's grace as the central reality of life. The disciplines of regular corporate worship, participation in Bible study, and prayer have traditionally been considered essential to Protestant spirituality.

When members of the Roman Catholic tradition talk about spiritual formation they mean the way in which the whole person is related to God. No aspect of life falls outside of consideration in the process of spiritual formation. Spiritual direction typically includes reflection through dialogue with reference to Scripture led by a spiritual director. The dialogue includes attention to the way sexual desire affects relationship with God. Protestants have practiced corporate spiritual formation, but there is no corporate equivalent to the attention given to sexuality as a part of Catholic spiritual direction. The sexuality of pastors and people is not usually a consideration in Protestant spiritual formation.

The purpose of Christian spiritual formation is growth in grace, or in capacity to live in faithful response to God's love. It assumes that each Christian has the potential to "grow up in every way into him who is the head, into Christ, from whom the whole body . . . as each part is working properly, promotes the body's growth in building itself up in love" (Eph. 4:15, 16). The central question addressed by spiritual formation is that of the loves—the desires, affections, the appetites—of the heart. It is reflected in Jesus' question to Peter: "Do you love me?" (John 21:15-19). Nourishing the capacity to love and express affection is the very center of Christian spirituality.

There is a lack of awareness, if not outright denial, among Protestants about the positive nature of sexual desire. This is the basis of love and affection in a community of Christians. Life in a congregation is often treated as if members and pastors are so "spiritual" when they are in church that they are not also and always sexual beings! The Protestant propensity to deny that pastors are sexual beings like everyone else leads to misuse of power and authority in the church.

Where the positive nature of sexual desire is denied, so is the destructive potential of suppressed desire. This kind of denial interferes with the capacity of a congregation or a denomination to deal realistically with sexual abuse of parishioners by clergy. People prefer to pretend this is not a common occurrence. To deny the importance of passion to the Christian life is to underestimate the human capacity to express desire in ways that can build up or tear down the Body of Christ.

In the church, as in all human groups, sexual attraction plays a role in all group relations. Where people feel and express affection for each other sexuality can be a positive power that helps bind the group together. Christians express love of God, in part, through their affection and care for one another. Something is terribly wrong in any congregation where there is no evidence of warm friendship between members.

A dualistic theology of the Christian life inevitably results in a disembodied spirituality. The denial of sexual feelings among church members makes it difficult to experience the power of any presence, including the presence of God. Not all ways of relating to God are equally healthy. Whenever the mode of relating does not involve heart, mind, and body it will be a less vital form of spirituality.

Spirituality is intimately related to sexuality because of the natural human desire to seek union with the object of love. The yearning for completion, for acceptance, for oneness with some "other" expressed in biblical images, Bible stories, in relational theology, and in hymns can reveal the inner connection between the experience of physical longing for union and the search for intimacy with God. Healthy spirituality acknowledges and incorporates the erotic element in our efforts to seek God.

Teens are especially sensitive to the physical aspect of spirituality because they are so acutely aware of their own changing bodies. Due to the power of newly discovered desire in the teen years, there is unusual receptivity to seeking friendship with Jesus through participation in community, dialogue with Scripture, and in prayer.

It is essential for all Christians, but especially teen members of a congregation, to realize that issues of sexual identity and sexual behavior are not separable from their capacity to love God and neighbor. Spiritual formation in the Protestant church can help teens come to terms with sexual identity. It can provide guidance for both heterosexual and homosexual Christians in choosing faithful expressions of sexual desire.

Where the longing for God is satisfied, human sexuality is

enriched because spiritual discipline gives form and direction to desire. The mystery of sexual union is heightened for partners who love each other "in Christ." Conversely, exaggerated or compulsive love of any kind is a sign of alienation from God, of a lack of spiritual direction.

Family idolatry is a tragically misdirected form of religious devotion. It involves a preference for the familiar over the unknown, the local over the universal, and treats the familiar and local as if they were absolute. When Christians direct reverence toward love of family without acknowledging the source of that love, they may imagine they are expressing reverence for Christ when they are, in fact, engaging in idolatry.[11]

# CHAPTER 6

# *Family-related Ethical Issues*

*E*ver since the sexual revolution of the 1960s, it has become less clear why Christians should or do marry. The moral values associated with "the family pew" have had less influence on the sexual ethics of youths born after 1960 than the same values had for earlier generations of Protestants. Generational differences have created heartache for many disappointed parents. The inability of many congregations to address the life experience of the post-sixties generation realistically could be one of the reasons that so many young adults who came of age in the 1970s and 1980s are not found in "the family pew."

The great liability of the ethical values associated with "the family pew" is the extent to which the modern family has depended on an intolerance of variety. The small family unit known as a *nuclear family* today is the typical family type of the modern era in Western cultures.[1] During the last two hundred years, identity has been associated more with the family unit than with larger social units like a congregation. Until the 1960s, personal identity—a concept unknown to biblical writers—had been highly dependent on family loyalty and conformity to family values. This general pattern has been intensified in American Protestant culture by the association of family values with Christian and American values. Parents who were reared to believe that the values of "the family pew" are the only option for Christians are confused when they discover that their children do not conform to those ethical values.

For first-century Christians, a commitment to the new life in Christ required them to evaluate family commitments and the role of law in their lives. Just as they were freed from unquestioning commitment to Jewish tradition and law, Christians today can be freed from uncritical devotion to the "laws" of "the family pew." Some of the most troubling aspects of changing attitudes about sexual behavior are issues related to whether and why anyone would marry. While Protestants may believe they should marry and have children, it is not clear why they feel this way.

### Marriage and the Sexuality of Single Adults

In the New Testament, marriage is considered desirable for most people. A good marriage between two Christians is expected to contribute to the spiritual stability of each partner (I Cor. 7:2). Just as individual Christians belong to the Body of Christ and are expected to seek the well-being of other members of a Christian community, so marriage is also intended to enhance the well-being of each partner. The sexual relationship between husband and wife is important because it has bearing on their other roles, in the church and in their work. In other words, a good marriage between Christians can contribute to positive spiritual formation.

While biblical attitudes about marriage are mixed, the New Testament does not support a family ideal in which failure to marry is considered a tragedy. However, because of the premium placed on descendants of the "children of Abraham" in the Jewish tradition, marriage was normative for most Christians, and women were expected to bear children. In the letter to Corinth, Paul somewhat reluctantly concedes that marriage is acceptable. Unlike attitudes today, he favored the single life on grounds that a single Christian is free to give single-minded devotion to God (I Cor. 7:34-40).

However, in a pastoral letter written several generations later, advice about who marries and why was revised in the light of a different situation. A "traditional" prohibition of remarriage for widows was revised lest the "natural desires" of young widows get stronger than "their devotion to Christ." The writer fears the possibility that the accepted teaching will be a stumbling block to faith and concludes it is better to revise the "tradition" than risk immoral practices that could reflect negatively on the community (I Tim. 5:4-16). In both cases, the issue is how the expression of "natural desires" will affect Christian faith and the Christian community.

All families are said to be created and sustained by God's grace (Eph. 3:14). For Christians, God's blessing can be experienced in marriage and family life. All love between those who live by faith in Jesus Christ is enhanced by the presence of gifts of the Spirit. But it does not follow that marriage is essential to the Christian life because Christians can experience God's grace in a marital relationship.

In spite of changing cultural attitudes about marriage, many Protestants today think it is abnormal not to marry. No one knows this better than single adults. Since it is no longer taken for granted that marriage is for everyone, Christians need to know why they might choose to marry.

Attitudes about marriage in the Judeo-Christian tradition are more practical than romantic. Nowhere is this practicality more obvious than in the creation myths of Genesis. Why did God create them male and female? So they won't be lonely. So they can be co-workers, caring for God's world. And so they can populate the earth (Gen. 2:18-22). These ideas about marriage are found in the household rules of Ephesians, but are adapted to the ethics of the new life in Christ.

Although marriage is not a Protestant sacrament, many Protestants experience their marriage as sacramental. A special kind of knowing "in Christ" can occur when a couple is drawn closer to God's mysterious, ineffable love through their love for each other. As physical union provides a metaphor for the union of Christ with the church, the sexual bond in marriage can enhance the sense that in God's love all that alienates has been overcome. To love each other "in Christ" is to love the Christ in each other.

The sexual bond in marriage can be an expression of oneness in the Body of Christ, but the experience of unity of spirit is not limited to marriage. To experience oneness in Christ is to glimpse for a moment the truth that God's eternal love is stronger than the bonds of death.

> The Other is present to us in an astonishing immediacy and openness so that there seems to be a commingling of beings in bonds of affection. . . . This moment never lasts. One cannot recapture or command those moments of self-disclosure and relationship when another self was almost undistinguished from one's own self.[2]

All friendship between those who are made new in the Spirit partakes of love that overcomes separation and loneliness. This is love that drives out fear and anxiety, love grounded in faith in God through Jesus Christ. To live the new life in Christ is to love one another in the household of God.

The life of Christians "at home" is expected to reflect the love Christians have for one another, but family relationships are quite different from all other expressions of love. When two people live together, they become aware of differences that alienate. Each one brings an old way of life into their new life together. Strange behavior and attitudes in the other can be bewildering, incomprehensible, and sometimes distressing. Personal likes, dislikes, habits, attitudes, and ways of thinking and valuing will be different. Even though two people grow together in marriage, there is never a time when they will fully comprehend each other.

The counsel of mutual subjection to each other "in Christ" is good advice for Christians who marry. Feminists who blame patriarchal attitudes in early Christian writings for the oppression of women today make too much of the differing instructions to husband and wife. In "the household rule" in Ephesians, wives are told to be subject to their husbands; husbands are told to love their wives as their own bodies. The instructions are given as examples of how to "be subject to one another out of reverence for Christ" (Eph. 5:21-33).

The point is that both husband and wife are to respect each other because both are members of the household of God. This is an example of the self-sacrificing quality of all Christian love. It means that those who live a new life in Christ give up all prior claims to special status. The subjection of a wife to a husband does not mean that women are expected to sacrifice personal well-being for other family members.

The writer of Ephesians has considerable respect for the mysterious nature of the sexual bond. The "rule" for a household conveys the responsibility of Christians to seek the well-being of each other in marriage as they would seek the well-being of other members of the Christian community.

In marriage, faith is tested and can be deepened. Although an appreciation of God's love can be deepened in any friendship between Christians, in marriage the partners are committed to seeking mutual well-being over time. This does not happen automatically. Marriage can be regarded as an expression of Christian spirituality that will flourish best when both partners are actively seeking spiritual direction through participation in a community of Christians.

Traditional ideals can lead to such high expectations about love in marriage that couples are bound to be disappointed. The more realistic biblical perspective on human nature makes it possible to realize that a marriage may not be a union in which personalities are well balanced. Or, depending on life circumstances, there is more unity between the partners at some times than others. This does not mean that the marriage cannot contribute to the well-being of each partner. It means that most people need friends in faith who understand and support their spirituality in times when their partner cannot or does not.

## Younger Adults, Sexuality, and Marriage

It is very difficult for most parents who became adults before 1960 to understand the attitudes of their children about work and love. Many expect their "grown" children to find suitable work and marry after high school or college as they did. But times have changed. Most young adults today do not have the same kind of life choices available to them that were available in the period of economic expansion after the Second World War.

While some social critics accuse youth of being lazy, indulgent, and narcissistic, others see cultural attitudes about work changing because of a transition from an industrial to a service culture. Vocational guidance counselors in public schools are not a fad. They are necessary in a time when young people do not seem to have clear-cut vocational options available to them.

How should the parents of single young adults respond to twenty-five- and thirty-year-old "children" who live lives so different from their own years as young adults? How should they respond when sons and daughters show no interest in marriage but are living with a "friend"? Parents are hurt or angry, but do not usually turn away a "child" who comes home after a divorce, between failed relationships, or for economic reasons.

These parents are justifiably concerned. In the Protestant tradition, work and marriage are considered the two primary areas of life in which faithfulness to God is learned and expressed. But, like the idea of self-fulfillment in marriage or family life, Americans have exalted ideals about self-fulfillment in work as well. Work has a place in Christian life, but it is not taken for granted that human work should or will be personally fulfilling.

The Victorian experience set the stage for continuing Protestant expectations of upward mobility as signs of God's grace. Despite the shock of the Great Depression, expectations of upward mobility were renewed in post-war economic optimism. The middle-class connection of work to prosperity and God's blessing means that Protestants have come to believe that work *should* be rewarding. Many young adults who inherited these expectations have discovered that there is no corresponding reality in the work available to them. Many never find work that matches their expectations, skills, or educational preparation. Most find that their work is not personally fulfilling.

Opportunities to find a suitable marriage partner are not much better than those of finding rewarding work. Cultural pluralism means that young adults do not experience the kind of Protestant homogeneity of moral and social values that their parents took for granted. It is difficult for them to locate "our kind of people" except possibly at church.

There is not much encouragement for young adults to establish enduring relationships in a culture where immediate gratification of desire—sexual and otherwise—is a constant media message. For young adults fortunate enough to find a suitable mate, the scarcity of work and continuing inflation make the establishment of a new household increasingly difficult. Many cannot afford to rent an apartment in a major city. The possibility of owning a house seems a far distant dream, if not an impossibility, to many young couples.

In addition to changes in economic circumstances that are not favorable to establishing a home in the young-adult years, traditional marriage ideals complicate the ability to make choices. It is not viable today to wait for "the right person." The homogeneity of small-town Protestant values of the older generation led to a mystique about God-given partners as well as God-given roles for men and women. In the popular mythology of the time, everyone knew that the purpose of dating around was to find "the right person" because "marriages are made in heaven." This is a romantic luxury that creates impossible expectations about happiness in marriage. It is also confusing to parents who do not understand why dating is no longer common practice.

In less prosperous and less romantic times, Christians have viewed marriage in more pragmatic terms as God's good gift of providing a partner with whom to work and live and make love. If, in the process, a man and a woman were less lonely and if their union issued in children, that was good. From this perspective a marriage between two Christians was not contingent on falling in love. The question asked by young adults in less romantic times was not "Do I love . . . ?" It was "Can I learn to love . . . ?"

## The Sexuality of Single Adults

Given the circumstances in which young adults come of age today, many are sexually experienced before marriage, if they marry. Research indicates that "nearly three-quarters of white women eighteen and nineteen had had sexual intercourse in 1988, up from 64 percent in 1982"; 76 percent of single women fifteen to forty-four years of age said they were sexually active.[3]

While Christian parents may rightly wish to prevent premature sexual experimentation and possibly disastrous relationships, a parent of a young adult actually has little control over the private life of grown "children." Parents cannot impose their moral code on their children any more than the government can stop abortions by making them illegal.

The parents of many young adults are imbued with an ethic of premarital chastity. The way of evaluating sexual practices with regard to marriage in the New Testament suggests that Christians should never assume that the particular moral code they inherited is the only possibility for acceptable Christian behavior.

The Bible has relatively little to say about premarital sexual relations as a subject in its own right. Prohibitions against adultery are designed to protect the family unit and refer to persons who are already married. Fornication, considered less serious than adultery in Jewish law, can refer to single persons. This includes incest, bestiality, rape, prostitution, and homosexuality. In the New Testament, apart from Paul's recommendation of celibacy, the single life was not a concern in cultures where most people were expected to marry. But, fornication did refer to any sexual relationship outside of marriage.

When Paul says that it is better to marry than to burn, this presupposes that marriage is a choice, not an obligation, for Christians. Jesus' condemnation of lust is an especially stringent teaching for modern sexually aware teens and young adults who live in a culture that literally throbs with libidinous energy (Matt. 5:27-30). They may "burn" with sexual desire, but have little possibility of entertaining marriage.

The best reason to advise celibacy to unmarried younger adults is the Christian insight that the corporate nature of the marriage covenant supports partners in their intention to seek mutual well-being. Christians who marry should be able to expect support for their intentions in a community of Christians. The very presence of the community can be a reminder of their commitment. The example of others who enjoy their marriage can encourage those who are newly wed to persevere.

A marriage ceremony recognizes an already existing relationship. It is the nature of the ceremony to make the commitment of the partners public. This element is missing for a couple who only "live together." A sexual relationship outside of marriage, whether it involves living together or not, will be more vulnerable if differences begin to come between the couple. They are not likely to have a community that cares enough about their future together to encourage them to persevere when the going gets rough, as it does in every marriage.

Just as there are no guarantees that a marriage ceremony will insure the faithfulness of one partner to the other, it should not be assumed that a lasting and faithful union is not possible outside of marriage. It may be more difficult to sustain mutual respect over time without communal support, but it can be done.

What does this say to unmarried adults about the expression of their sexual desires? There are circumstances in which a man and a woman have a lasting relationship, one which is faithful by Christian standards, but find it not expedient to marry. This happens more often with older adults. Sometimes a younger couple does not or cannot marry but has a stable relationship over time. Is it better to burn with sexual desire than engage in a sexual relationship that cannot or may not lead to marriage (I Cor. 7:8-10)?

In the teachings of both Paul and Jesus, sexual desire that distracts Christians from being able to give their lives to "love and serve the Lord" is to be avoided. What does this suggest to unmarried younger adults who may have very little opportunity to marry? Is it better for them to burn with sexual desire than risk a sexual relationship that may not lead to marriage? Here, as in different positions regarding the remarriage of widows in the New Testament, the issue is whether this union will enhance faithfulness to God.

On what grounds can official church teaching continue an absolute prohibition of all nonmarital sexual relationships? New Testament attitudes about the expression of sexuality—and what happens when people try to repress sexual desire—seem more realistic and more merciful than current Protestant teaching would indicate.

There is a difference between a more accepting attitude about sexual relationships outside of marriage and advocacy of "free love"! It is possible to accept an alternative expression of sexuality without implying that it is good for everyone. There are very good reasons for Christians to know why they marry and how that choice is related to the life of faith. It would be helpful if more Christians were aware of the benefits of the corporate nature of the marriage covenant. But knowing that Christians may have options might ease the pain of parents who feel that the sexual behavior of their children is a rejection of everything they stand for.

Several denominations now recommend "celibacy in single-ness and fidelity in marriage."[4] If taken seriously by unmarried Christians, this can encourage suppression of sexual desire to avoid breaking a moral law. It is possible for unmarried lovers to practice celibacy, but is it spiritually helpful? Paul warned that trying to practice celibacy in marriage could lead to infidelity on the part of one of the partners. Is it better for young adults to practice celibacy in singleness when they "burn with desire"? An ethic that does not ask how keeping the "law" affects the spirit of the persons involved is not a law of love.

Christian parents may be more understanding of the life-style of their children if they realize that the world in which their children have come of age requires their children to make decisions about sexual behavior that were not even issues in the past. Everyone has a need for physical intimacy and compan-ionship in daily life. Given present cultural circumstances, younger adults find a variety of ways to satisfy their longing for intimacy and friendship. Some create a surrogate family. Some live with friends who are not lovers. Some live with lovers who are friends.

There is considerable variation in the living arrangements of both unmarried heterosexual and homosexual couples. Homosexual couples who want to commit themselves to a monogamous lifelong relationship find themselves in the same situation as anyone else who cohabits without benefit of marriage. The difference is that there is no choice for homosexuals.

The possibility that a gay or lesbian relationship might be a "marriage" is so alien to current attitudes about homosexuality that there is no language and no publicly accepted ritual to acknowledge their intentions. Yet, they, as much as anyone else, are in need of corporate witness and support for their commitment.

When two Christians live together in a relationship that is not a marriage, for whatever reasons, the commitment of the relationship can be evaluated the same way the commitment in a marriage between Christians is evaluated. Does the love expressed between these two people support the ability of each to live the Christian life of love more fully?

## Parenthood as a Ministry

There are a good many parents who wish they were grandparents. Couples who do not choose to become parents and couples who are unable to become parents may find themselves being subtly pressured by parents or peers. It is hard for the older generation to accept the fact that parenthood is now subject to choice, especially when it means that they may never have grandchildren. Some respond to this situation as if they have no future life unless their bloodline is continued through their children.

This legacy of the American Dream still conveys a sense that if a woman is not a mother, she is not complete. These attitudes are particularly cruel in the case of couples who spend a great deal of time and money trying to conceive. But faithful following of Jesus in the gospel is not described in terms of a family obligation to procreate. The best friends of Jesus—Mary, Martha, and Lazarus—were single young adults!

In the past, dualistic thinking about what it means to be a woman so strongly associated motherhood with women that childbearing seemed essential to spiritual wholeness. Since birth control has become easily available, it is possible to ask whether all Christian couples should become parents. On what grounds should a couple decide that it would be faithful to their calling as Christians to become parents?

Protestants have always believed that being parents is a God-given calling, even though they have not always believed it unnatural to be single or childless. Traditionally, Protestants have said that parenthood is work given by God, and that it is a service to human society. That is why all work, including that of parenthood, is to be done "as to the Lord."

Attitudes about a division of labor between men and women make it difficult to think of men as parents by closely associating parenthood with mothers. In the Victorian period, the identity of women was so strongly dependent on the bearing and rearing of children that men often felt shut out of family life. Many still do, especially in homes where women do not work outside of the home.

The expectation that a man should support his family financially continues to suggest that the "right" place for men is in the work world, while "real" women give themselves in service to family and church. This unfortunate dualism continues to influence attitudes about what it means to be a man and a woman even though over half of the working women in the United States are working to support a family.

Many church members continue to feel that the God-given role of women is in "the Christian home," as "the keepers of the springs." As long as parenthood was not a choice, modern Protestants rarely asked about the work of women. It can no longer be taken for granted that all women will or should become mothers.

*Parenthood as a Servant Ministry*

Every Christian has a vocation, a calling to some particular work in the world, given as their service to God. There are no gender-specific vocations. Men and women are both called to perform work that contributes to the good of God's world. There are two purposes for Christian callings. First, all work contributes to the well-being of the world. Second, the work of Christians in the world is a form of evangelism. For Christians, parenthood is both an act of faith and a servant ministry.

Parenthood is not for everyone. Freedom in Christ means freedom from uncritical allegiance to social conventions. A Christian man can choose not to be a slave to career ambition so that he can devote enough time to being a good father. No Christian woman has to assume that the only or best work to which she is called by God is that of being a wife and mother. There are childless couples who can, in good faith, conclude that the present work of each is their proper and full calling. Some division of labor between home and work is necessary for every couple, whether they are parents or not. There is no single arrangement that is right for everyone.

Just as a good marriage requires personal change and sacrifice of both partners, so does parenthood. New parents find that the inclusion of a third person in their home and their lives reduces privacy and changes daily living habits. A man and a woman establish a new relationship with each other while learning to care for their child together. In the process, one or both of them may find it necessary to give up some personal ambition, work projects, or free time.

In this time of cultural confusion about the meaning of family life, the world needs to see the kind of attitudes Christians can bring to their family relationships and responsibilities. The corporate nature of the Christian life means that parents should be able to find support and encouragement for their work as parents among other members of their congregation. Sometimes it is hard to remember that the drudgery or pain involved in being responsible for a baby, a child, or a teen is a labor of love. Sometimes it seems like all of the effort has come to nothing. Remembering that parenthood is a servant ministry can be an aid to faith.

Parents who try to rear children in "the discipline and instruction of the Lord" without support from a Christian community will not find family life easier; they will find it more difficult. The attitudes that Christian parents want for their children are not always the same as the attitudes of the rest of the world. Membership in a Christian community offers them companionship in work that will test their faithfulness, patience, and perseverance. Regular worship, Bible study, and prayer are aids to faith, especially as these disciplines remind Christian parents of the presence of God's grace in all of life.

### Divorce and Reconciliation

Divorce is now so common that some couples commit themselves to a marriage for only "as long as love shall last." Few extended families have been untouched by the phenomenal increase in divorce in the last twenty years. Attitudes about divorce in the church have changed to fit the new situation. Less than thirty years ago, Presbyterian polity instructed pastors not to perform a marriage ceremony if the man or woman had ever been divorced. The reason for this policy was considered biblical.

Although it is now less common to absolutely prohibit divorce, there are still congregations and denominations where divorce is prohibited on biblical grounds. Even where divorce is acceptable, many Christians who have been divorced in recent years feel that they have failed. Some associate their sense of failure with the church so strongly that they may feel unwelcome in their congregation. They may feel unacceptable to God as well as to members of their congregation.

Divorce is tragic. Divorce often seems like the end of life because of the intense alienation that usually is involved. Like marriage, divorce has a public dimension that touches the lives of all who know the couple. It is not unusual for others to feel threatened when friends or family members divorce. The fact that divorce is now so common may fuel the belief that marriage is so difficult that it might not last for a lifetime. Friends and family members may want to avoid a couple in trouble at the very time they most need encouragement.

The Matthean account of Jesus' reflection about divorce and Jewish law suggests that the spiritual dimensions of a divorce are important. People who divorce may experience it as the end of their fondest hopes and dreams. But divorce is more than the end of a dream, more than the inability to keep a commitment. Divorce feels like the end of life because a union in which two became one has dissolved. A part of the self seems to be lost. Some people never recover their self-respect after a divorce. Others find it difficult to trust because an intimacy has been betrayed.

A divorce wounds the spirit in ways that are difficult to anticipate. It is a time when people need to know that they are forgiven and that they can forgive. In some congregations, a divorce between two members is acknowledged by a rite of confession. The intention of the ritual is to confess failure on the part of the couple and the congregation so that healing can occur. This seems to be a good idea, but it may trivialize the consequences of divorce for the couple and for the congregation.

When two Christians mutually agree that they no longer have a marriage, it is a genuine tragedy that should be repented. If they have made serious attempts with the help of a pastor or counselor to reconcile their differences, they may conclude that a divorce is preferable to living with alienation.[5] The "sin" involved is not the decision to divorce; it is the experience of alienation from God, self, and others that causes damage to the human spirit.

The ebb and flow of marriage is bound to have periods in which mutual concern and respect is strained by other interests and other loves. Infidelity takes different forms for people . . . excessive love of work, of children, or of another person. The importance of forgiveness in a Christian marriage—knowing that the past can be left behind—can hardly be overestimated when temptations to unfaithfulness are so common.

Pastors are particularly vulnerable to the temptations of excessive work and adultery. A recent study funded by the Lilly Endowment indicates that one in four clergy has had some kind of sexual contact with a parishioner and one in ten has had an affair with a parishioner.[6] The extent of clergy adultery and clergy divorce is fair indication that unfaithfulness in marriage is also fairly common.

When clergy are known to be involved with someone in their congregation, or when clergy divorce, the effect on the congregation is considerably more serious than the ramifications for the congregation when members divorce. The sexual contact of a pastor with a parishioner is considered sexual abuse from the standpoint of professional ethics. This raises a larger issue for the church concerning the spirituality of pastors and the people entrusted to their care.

*Forgiveness and Reconciliation*

There are times in most marriages when mutual respect is shattered and forgiveness seems impossible. Yet, an attitude of forgiveness is part of what it means for Christians to love one another. This is not easily learned or practiced in a culture where it is beneficial to have power over other people. Reconciliation will be very difficult if not impossible when only one party is willing to admit failure and begin again.

If a marriage ends in divorce, everyone involved will suffer some loss of self-respect. If children are involved, the parents usually experience guilt over their inability to keep the family together. Yet, the admission of inability to be faithful to the marriage covenant is the first step in a healing process. Confession of failure is an act in which the healing power of God's forgiving mercy can be discovered. This, too, is difficult in a culture in which it is more common to blame others than to accept responsibility for failure.

A broken relationship is always a faith issue. Although it is not always obvious, people who divorce lose faith in themselves. In a case where one or both will not forgive, their ability to trust God, self, and others is diminished.

The same thing seems to happen when a congregation is disappointed by a pastor. The failure of church judicatories to confront the unfaithfulness of a pastor—when the pastor's unfaithfulness is common knowledge in the congregation—robs members of an opportunity for healing. If the pastor's supervisor refuses to acknowledge that there is a problem, then it is impossible for the congregation to deal with the spiritual issues involved. This makes it difficult for members to trust new leaders and one another.

Members of a congregation may need to make special efforts to help newly divorced people realize that the community is a place where faith can be restored. The healing of broken persons is a process of learning to trust again; it is a process of learning to respect self and others again. It is learning to believe that there is new life in Christ. A rite of reconciliation does not restore respect, but it can represent the beginning of new life for those who repent and believe.

When the trust of a congregation has been violated, it is the responsibility of the larger Christian community to realize that it may be necessary for members of the congregation to be forgiven and reconciled to one another.

Adults who divorce are sometimes referred to as "single again." They may be treated differently from a widow or a widower, and in some ways they are different. But any adult who is "single again" for any reason is bound to be lonely. Whether newly divorced or newly widowed, there is a period of grief. For both, there is some experience of guilt. Programs for adults who are single or "single again" often fail to give enough attention to the reality that life is shattered when a companion is lost. It is difficult for congregations to recognize the variety of needs experienced by people who are single again, especially those of a single parent.[7]

The mystique of "the ideal family" can obscure the extent to which all kinds of families need spiritual support from the church. It also obscures the capacity to realize that some members of every congregation experience family life as a nightmare. It is now known that family disorganization and abusive domestic relationships are common in middle-class families. This reality will not get the attention it deserves unless pastors are able to see that there are no ideal families.[8]

Church programs in the post-war era were designed to serve members of "healthy," intact families. They were organized on the premise that most members learn to love in "the Christian home." This attitude cannot do justice to the deeply human need for forgiveness and reconciliation in all relationships.

There are no families untouched by strain between generations. There are no marriages in which there will not be misunderstanding between marital partners. There are no members of any congregation who do not need to know the power of Christ's forgiving love in their lives.

*The Family Life of Pastors*

The marital commitments and family life of pastors are no less troubling or complicated than those of laity.[9] The double calling of most Christians to career and to family life means that all Christians, including those who are ordained church leaders, should be able to expect the church to support them in their life commitments.

In the Protestant tradition, clergy and laity are both expected to express faithfulness to God through faithfulness to family responsibilities. Yet, the nature of clergy responsibility in the church today is such that many pastors find an imbalance between commitment to ministry and faithfulness to family. It is rare to find a pastor who does not experience conflict between these two loyalties. It is ironic that pastors may respond to expectations about family-related pastoral care in their congregations at the expense of their own family relationships.

Current congregational practices often deny that all members are to work together to "build up the Body of Christ." One of the reasons pastors often neglect their own families is that the demand for pastoral care of families has increased in recent years. A pastor is expected to see that all of the people of God do the work of the church, not to do the work of the church on behalf of the people of God. Thus, part 3 is about the servant role of a pastor as the spiritual director of a congregation.

# PART THREE

# The Pastor as Spiritual Director of a Congregation

# CHAPTER 7

# *New Life in the Congregation*

*E*vidence indicates that Protestant ways of thinking about the church, family, and sexuality have lost meaning and may actually interfere with the capacity of church members to respond to change in the family. The family as a social institution is not extinct. The Protestant ideal of family is inadequate when dealing with life in a changing culture and can mislead the thinking of pastors about Christian spirituality.

Even though the Bible is an ancient book, it offers ways of thinking about the world that can still be considered a guide to Christian faith. The general attitudes and ordering of values in Scripture contain timeless wisdom about God's relationship to the people of God and the world. When viewed as a general guide to faith rather than as a collection of specific teachings, the Bible can provide a basis for theological reflection and dialogue about every aspect of life for contemporary Christians.

### "Family Pew" Illusions and Spiritual Formation

Changes in family life affect all church programs, from habits of worship to women's associations. Response to these changes is not likely to have much long-range impact on the life of a congregation if the traditional "Sunday School and Church" program structure is not evaluated first. A recent study of "effective Christian education" by Search Institute concluded that:

> Christian education in a majority of congregations is a tired enterprise in need of reform. Often out-of-touch with adult and adolescent needs, it experiences increasing difficulty in finding and motivating volunteers, faces general disinterest among its "clients," and employs models and procedures that have changed little over time.[1]

With a few notable exceptions, most congregations are still organized as if the premise of "the family pew" is true—that church members are Christian because they learn Christian attitudes at home, knowledge of the Bible in Sunday School, and attend worship regularly. The leadership structure in most congregations operates as if a three-way division of labor between parents, Sunday School teachers, and pastors still exists and is adequate to the spiritual formation of children and youth.

If "Sunday School and Church" is the formative experience in a congregation, it is very likely that the people of God are being formed by a structure that perpetuates dualistic thinking about Christian faith, about the work of Christians, the nature of the church, and the role of pastors. This once vital tradition was more effective when Protestant values were more dominant in American culture than they are now. But the very nature of the division of spiritual formation of Christians between lay leaders in the Sunday School and pastoral leaders in the church leaves people with the idea that Christian faith can be learned by attending classes.

At one time, Protestants were more familiar with biblical language and the content of the Bible than they are today. Many learned to pray by attending weekly prayer meetings. Regular Sunday evening services were used for hymn singing, Bible study, and social ministry concerns. When the churches were the social center in small towns and villages across the country, it was not uncommon for whole families to attend worship services two or three times a week.

Where the older cultural patterns are more intact, the Sunday

School is better able to function as a school where people learn about the Bible. However, knowledge about the Bible is only the first stage in learning to reflect about life in the light of Scripture. The use of the Bible as a guide to faith for a congregation is a lifelong learning process that can be practiced every time members gather as a congregation.

As the person set aside by a congregation to be their spiritual leader, the pastor is the person most responsible for interpreting the life of faith in the light of Scripture. This means more than interpreting Scripture in sermons. It means that the people need to learn how to reflect about their lives and the life of the congregation in the light of Scripture. One of the ways a pastor can help people learn to think biblically is through leading Bible study groups. Another is by opening all church-related meetings with Bible study, meditation, and prayer. This is not just the pastor's responsibility, but if the pastor does not model this kind of Scripture use, the people cannot be expected to exhibit these attitudes and practices.

All of the work of the congregation—the committee meetings, the youth groups, teacher training meetings—are occasions for Bible study and meditation guided by Scripture. This use of "biblical knowledge" is practiced in congregations where members understand that Christian faith is a way of life that includes a personal sense of responsibility for the welfare of others, both in the congregation and in the world. In these congregations, there is a connection between:

> education content that blends biblical knowledge and insight with significant engagement in the major life issues each age group faces. Effective adult education emphasizes biblical knowledge, multicultural and global awareness, and moral decision making. Emphases for youth include sexuality, drugs and alcohol, service and friendship.[2]

Curriculum writers, Christian educators, and pastors should know from experience that finding better curriculum material for Sunday School teachers does not transform persons. Yet, it is tempting to get caught up in the hope that it is *only* the print curriculum that needs to be changed. Denominations encourage this illusion in their continuing efforts to produce and market a new curriculum every three to four years—sometimes without even evaluating the effect of the old curriculum on learners. By itself, a curriculum has very little impact on learners. That is due, in part, to who the learners are. It is also due to the way curriculum is used by teachers and to whether the teachers are communicating faith to their students.

All aspects of church life educate people about the life of faith. Technically, *curriculum* refers to running a course, as in following a preset course in a race to its end. The pastor, the person charged with giving order to the life of a congregation, sets the course in a congregation. This suggests that the pastor's role as spiritual leader is to make an intentional effort to help the people live in faithful response to God. This includes attention to their way of thinking about life; to their use and understanding of the Bible; to the influence of their teachers, friends, and family; and to what they can learn about relationships from life in the congregation.

When the pastor's responsibility is seen as the spiritual formation of a congregation, this means that the pastor will be concerned with the purpose of every part of the life of the congregation. The various educational ministries are essential to spiritual formation, but education for faith is not limited to what happens in Sunday School. In most congregations, Sunday School has outlived its original functions, but that does not mean that it cannot be revitalized. With leadership from the pastor, Sunday School can be an introduction to Christian spirituality through learning about the Bible and Christian tradition.

The following questions can be used to assess the present quality of spiritual formation in a congregation. They are indicative of a general approach to spiritual formation in which the Sunday School is only one part.

1. Where do members learn to love the Word of God? Are they learning the content and meaning of Scripture? Are they learning what it means for them, the church, and the world?

2. Are teachers able to convey their own faith in Jesus Christ by their attitudes and actions, by the way they teach?

3. Is the congregation a place where people know that they are loved by God because members care about one another and are able to forgive one another?

4. When church members gather, is prayer a natural part of their life together?

5. Do children and younger persons learn attitudes characteristic of Christians from being with the adults in this congregation? Do ways of relating, concerns expressed, and work done express attitudes of goodness, kindness, peace, and joy?

6. From whom do congregation members of all ages learn that every Christian has gifts for ministry, that their service to others is essential to faith?

People learn from what they hear, what they see, and what they do. There are many reasons why people attend church. Despite all appearances to the contrary and misunderstandings about the nature of the church, members are looking for God. Most people want a pastor who can help them reflect on their need for God. They need a pastor who can help them see the presence of God's grace in life, someone who encourages them to express their faith. This is the purpose of every gathering in a congregation. The work agenda will differ, but the point of gathering is always an expression of love of God and neighbor.

When the people of God gather in a congregational setting, they are being formed into a people of God through participation in worship, study, fellowship, and mission. These activities are not optional to Christian spirituality; each one is necessary to a full experience and expression of faith in Jesus Christ. Participation in each area is not limited to one age-group only. From early childhood to late adulthood, Christian faith is best learned and expressed when people are active in worship, study, fellowship, and mission.

*Spiritual Formation Through Liturgy*

A spiritual imbalance will inevitably exist in a congregation where members are not expected to be as spiritually disciplined as the pastor. Role confusion in a church is more than an inequality of power between pastors and people. It is not just a difference of opinion over decision making in a congregation. The deeper issue is the genuine spiritual power recognizable in a pastor who, as the spiritual guide of a congregation, has faithfully practiced the traditional disciplines of Christian faith. The issue is not just which ministry belongs to laity and which ministry belongs to the pastor. The real issue is far more basic. It is a question of how people become intentionally Christian in their life orientation, attitudes, and values.

In a congregation where most adults are not committed to study or to regular worship, the pastor may be the only adult who is regularly nourished and challenged by Scripture. Every member needs similar opportunities for spiritual formation. Just as pastoral care is the work of all members of the congregation, so is regular study and preparation for worship.

The Word of God comes alive as a congregation hears the Word in worship and preaching, learns what the Word is about through study, and discovers what the Word means as it is experienced through life in a fellowship of Christians. It is in hearing and experiencing the meaning of the good news through regular participation in corporate life that people begin to see and think differently about life.

Educational programs in many congregations proceed on the unexamined premise that Christian faith is formed in the hearts of little children and young people through the influence of "the Christian home." This overlooks the formative power of the church as the first family of Christians where teens and adults from all kinds of families can experience the quality of love and forgiveness they need to sustain family life. This kind of faithfulness to family commitments is facilitated through liturgy that gives order and meaning to the lives of church members.

People are formed by the repeated acts that give meaning to their lives, by the events that touch their hearts.[3] Weekly worship is a time when members can bring their lives before God. In addition to the gratitude, joy, suffering, or sorrow that they bring to worship each week, members of families also come to worship with hurt or resentment from family disagreements and differences. They should be able to get perspective on themselves through participation in Word and Sacrament. Commitments are renewed, wounds are healed, and disappointments are left behind when people go away from the fellowship of Christian sisters and brothers. Fellowship is a reminder of God's love.

Rituals mark the passage of time. They are markers that measure the meaning of a life. The seasons of the Christian year—Advent, Christmas, Lent, Easter, and Pentecost—can give form across the years of a lifetime to the predictable events of life.

The recovery of worship organized around the seasons of the church year among Protestants may be a healthy sign of movement away from family life-cycle events as the major concern in the worship of a congregation. When the calendar of the church year governs the themes of worship and the selection of sermon topics throughout the year, the people of God can reflect on the events of their lives according to the moods of the seasons of the church year. When the seasons of the church year set the mood for corporate worship, events in the life of Jesus become the prism through which all else is reflected.[4] But when the civic calendar and family-life celebrations govern the worship of a congregation, it is much more difficult for the pastor to convey what it means to reflect about all of life in the light of the life and teaching of Jesus Christ.

Christian spiritual disciplines are learned through experience and practice. All Christians need to know what they believe. But what they believe may not become integrated into lives lived in relationship with God if they do not worship regularly. The meaning of *new life in Christ* can never be exhausted for believers. The experience of new life is formed and reformed as all of life is looked at and interpreted with reference to the various movements in the life of faith, ritualized every year in the celebrations of the church—Christmas, Easter, Pentecost.

Keeping the seasons of the church year gives tempo, theme, rhythm, and balance to the lives of the faithful. The message of new life in Christ is always the same—that those who believe have been given new life through the sacrifice of Jesus Christ. Regardless of what is happening among biological kin in any given week, members of the Body of Christ are helped by remembering that God loves and forgives them as they participate in the incarnation; the birth, death, and resurrection of Jesus Christ; the birth of the church; and the giving of the Holy Spirit.

As is the case with the language of spiritual formation, some Protestant pastors have an aversion to keeping the seasons of the church year. Some believe that Catholics and Episcopalians make an idol of a liturgical form of worship. But any worship form can become an empty ritual valued only because it is familiar. When loyalty to civic and family values interferes with loyalty to Jesus Christ, serious consideration should be given to the possibility that a nonliturgical, so-called "free" worship tradition may reinforce "family pew" loyalties.

When observed with regularity, the celebration of the sacraments can be time of renewal, a time that marks new movements in the life of faith. As visible signs of God's love and forgiveness, baptism and the Supper can extend the horizons of believers from limited visions of the church as local and particular toward a sense that they belong to the whole communion of saints. The baptismal water, the bread and the cup, are present reminders that Christians are called out, cleansed, and constantly renewed as they participate in the eternal love of God through their membership in the Body of Christ.

Like worship, the sacraments may seem like dead rituals in the life of the church today. But where the hearts of believers feel gratitude for the great sacrifice of Jesus Christ, the Supper can seem like union with Christ. The Lord's Supper is the time in the life of a congregation when the power of God's love to overcome the forces of evil and death is held up to eyes of faith. It is *the* corporate celebration of God's love, in which all isolation and differences are—for a moment—overcome.

The liturgy of Word and Sacrament is a form through which the Spirit can breath new life into the people of God. The repetition of prayer, Scripture, hymns, and sacraments over a lifetime—or some part of it—can take root in the heart. The words, the music, a particular way of seeing the world can become part of the life of a congregation.

The Christian way of ordering life through liturgy is not likely to establish the themes and rhythms of the lives of members unless they are in the habit of regular worship. Members who worship sporadically are much less likely to be able to see the world in a new way, given the power of intellectual, moral, and social values of the world in which they live most of their lives.

## Planning for New Life in the Congregation

The work of a pastor can be described as responsibility for Word, Order, and Sacrament in the life of a congregation. Historically, this meant giving order, or spiritual direction, to the life of a congregation. Today, *order* usually refers to church administration. The only reason for church administration is to organize a congregation so that members will be able to express and experience the power of God's grace in their lives.

There is strong evidence that the focus of spiritually alive congregations is the ministry of all Christians. Where the pastor clearly articulates the purpose and identity of a congregation, members know what it is and understand that they have a place in the mission of the congregation.[5] Where a congregation lacks a sharply defined mission, members may serve on committees and attend meetings for which they can state no purpose. Programs and committee structures can continue for generations simply because they are the local tradition.

There is a connection between the way people understand their church-related work and the importance they attach to worship. If members do not relate church-work to their own spiritual formation, there is no pressing need for them to worship. The way a congregation is organized can work against positive spiritual formation. It is not unusual for people to complete a term of service on a board and then disappear. They say they are "burned out." *Why?* Many Sunday School teachers do not worship regularly. *Why not?*

Many congregations have trouble finding volunteers to staff

traditional church programs. Some say that there are fewer willing workers because so many women work. However, that doesn't explain common attitudes about church-work. Some people regard their church work as one more civic duty. Parents take turns teaching Sunday School as they take turns being Scout leaders. Members may regard election to office in a congregation as a reward for service in less important leadership capacities.

This is not to say that no one in a congregation thinks of their church-work as stewardship to God. Hierarchical attitudes about the importance and power associated with different kinds of church-work make it difficult for pastors to convey the idea that different gifts for ministry are suited to different offices.

Ministry in the congregation *can* be an expression of faith, but for many it may only be church-work. A task-oriented, businesslike approach to church administration may get work done. But why does anyone do the work of a congregation? The church consists of people who need to know God's love for them far more than they need more work to do. It is important for a pastor to be aware of what happens to the faith of members as they participate in leadership positions in a congregation. Pastors and people are formed by the work they do. For both, church-work can be a contribution to the life of a congregation, an expression of their faith. But it can also be only an uncritical repetition of local tradition.

It is one thing to be aware of the way attitudes have been shaped by dualistic thinking about Christian faith. It is another to try to change attitudes and values. People can change if they are helped to appreciate how their faith is limited by old ways of thinking. This can happen when they begin to see their world in a new way because of positive experiences with others in the ongoing life of a congregation. It also happens because the way they think about Christian faith is changing.

Program structure is difficult to change because congregations *are* complacent about "the way we always do it here." It may not be as important to change present programs as it is to change the way people think about the programs. Dualistic ways of thinking about what is spiritual and what is not affects the way people act and relate in a congregation.

Members of every congregation have traditional ways of relating to one another. There are unwritten rules about what can and cannot be discussed in church.[6] Dualistic attitudes about what is and is not spiritual or religious are operative if sexuality is not considered a polite topic of conversation among church members. There are other less obvious social conventions that influence what can and cannot happen when the people gather as the church. Often, people who know one another socially do not discuss the same subjects in church that they would discuss anywhere else. Many express themselves in ways they perceive as being more religious when they are in church. In short, some people pretend to be someone else when they come to church!

There is a convention in many congregations that family life is a private affair. Some members want the pastor to call only when they have a family problem. Others keep anything that goes wrong with a family member secret. It is one thing to understand that family ideals can be idolatrous. It is another to wonder how the deeply embedded values about family privacy are changed.

Lack of intimacy among members of a congregation is a common problem. The observation is often made that people who worship together do not know one another. It is then suggested that members of a congregation will have better fellowship if they have more contact. This is probably true, but planning more activities is not the answer. People can get acquainted through fellowship activities without developing a personal sense of responsibility for one another as "brothers and sisters in Christ." As long as there are unspoken conventions that keep members from being friends who can tell one another about life at home and at work, it will be almost impossible for a pastor to convey to them that Christian faith affects all areas of life, all moral and social values.

For example, there are parents in every congregation who are desperately unhappy about the sexual behavior of a "child." The church may be the last place they think of asking for help.

Even when other families have had similar experiences, members cannot encourage one another if the home life of members is considered private. A congregation may offer an occasional course on sexuality for teens, adults, or both, but the issue is more than whether members would attend classes to learn about their sexuality. The larger issue is that of secrecy about life in "the Christian home."

*Changing the Topic of Conversation*

Pastors may not be aware of the extent to which they influence topics of conversation in congregations through the subjects they discuss in sermons and worship. If a pastor is comfortable talking about all aspects of human life, this gives the people permission to discuss everything that touches their lives when they gather. When a sermon includes attention to some previously overlooked or taboo subject, members can see that everything that happens in the world is of concern to Christians. Too often, it is the most important events in life that members feel they must leave outside the door of the sanctuary.

A recent study of sermons preached after World War II shows that there were common themes and perspectives in the sermons of that period. Both liberals and conservatives presupposed a vision of the kingdom of God but differentiated the vision from concrete realities. According to Robert Wuthnow, this way of spiritualizing religious vision distanced the religious discourse of the church from personal life and influenced sermon topic selection.

In liberal preaching this had the effect of preaching a vision of the Kingdom that created a mood of expectancy, of working toward something grand; but it reduced the life of faith to symbolic spiritual activity. Conservative preaching included such mundane topics as work, family life, and church programs; but they were treated in terms of utopian visions—getting rich, always being happy, finding the perfect church.[7]

This spiritualizing of daily life still influences preaching. For instance, it is remarkable how little attention is given to the effects of alcohol, drugs, and tranquilizers on the lives of church members. Silence about such subjects only reinforces the unhealthy tendency of Protestants to relegate family problems to a private realm. Sexual behavior and substance abuse are not just moral issues; they are issues of the human spirit that beg for corporate theological reflection.

If members of a congregation do not see sexuality as a spiritual issue, there is little likelihood that they will see that domestic violence, homosexuality, and AIDS are issues that affect their lives. That is why members of congregations are so prone to imagine that most social problems affect some other group but not "our kind of people."

Social conventions about privacy in the family encourage hypocrisy and cause unnecessary suffering, all in the name of the sanctity of the family. These attitudes affect the family life of pastors as well but often in the opposite way. Since pastors are perceived as belonging to a more public realm, pastors often have the impression that their family life is not private. Yet, members of a congregation may be fully aware that there is a problem in the pastor's family without ever offering sympathy or assistance. All family-related problems are likely to remain in the private realm of pastoral care unless pastors end the conspiracy of silence about what really happens in the family life of members, without breaking confidences.

## A Unified Vision of Ministry

The model of ministry as spiritual direction of the life of a congregation assumes that the gospel comes alive when addressed to life realities. This does not mean that church members do not now experience new life in Christ as they participate in the life of a congregation. But pastors should realize that they and their members may think about Christian faith in ways that obscure whole realms of experience. When important parts of life are not subject to theological reflection, people are not able to believe that God's grace really is at work there.

Christian feminists have contributed to knowledge about the ways in which dualistic theologies function to deprive women and minorities of power and authority in the church. This knowledge can help clear the way for learning to see reality in ways that more accurately reflect the acts and attitudes of Jesus. Dualistic thinking affects everyone, not just women and members of minority groups. Pastors and people—men and women—are robbed of new life in Christ by the ways in which dualistic thinking impacts the life of a congregation.

If members of a congregation can see that the forces of good and evil in the world affect *everyone* in *some* way, but not the *same* *way,* then they may realize that *all* problems are *human* problems. A dualistic view of the world and the church leads church people to believe that other people have problems different from their own. Many attempts to engage a congregation in ministry to "the less fortunate" fail because of a belief that "they" should be like "us." A congregation that is able to see its ministries as service to God probably has a pastor who has helped people to recognize that *why* they do something is as important as *what* they do.

The purpose of evangelism in New Testament congregations was not to make everyone the same; it was to offer everyone new life in Christ. Congregations cared about the well-being of members not so that everyone would conform to the same moral and social values, but because Christians are expected to respect their brothers and sisters for whom Christ died. Christians are called to give service to one another and to the world because they are free in Christ to recognize the integrity of every human being.

The Bible can be the book of the church if members are able to bring all of life to the mirror of Scripture for reflection about the life of faith. In more traditional language, this is the practice of spiritual discernment.

## Reform of Membership Rituals

The way people talk about their church is indicative of how they think about Christianity and what it means for them to be Christian. People say they are going to "join a church." This means they belong to a congregation, which may or may not be considered a part of the Church universal. When members are considered *active* or *inactive,* this usually refers to worship and pledging habits.

When teens join a church, they usually do so after attending a confirmation class. There is a new ritual in which adults renew their baptismal vows. Strictly speaking, if they were baptized as infants, they cannot "renew" vows made by someone else on their behalf. This language about baptism and church membership suggests that the church is only one activity among many. Yet, the fact that people are attracted to baptismal renewal is a sign that they are looking for rituals that have more spiritual significance for their lives than those already available in a congregation.

## Confirmation: Earning a Seat in "the Family Pew"

When an infant is baptized, some pastors tell the congregation that the baby is now your brother or sister in Christ. This means that the baby is now a member of the Church universal. A confirmation class supposedly prepares young people to confirm vows made on their behalf if they were baptized as infants. This is understood as choosing church membership for themselves.

According to this way of thinking, teens become "real" church members through confirmation. They are expected to emerge from a relatively short learning experience as fully responsible "adult" members who are committed to ministry in Jesus' name. This suggests that these young people have made a decision and are—in the words of the Bible—confessing belief that Jesus Christ is Lord. People continue to believe this even though in many congregations it is common knowledge that many teens drop out of the congregation almost as soon as they have been confirmed.

In Protestant traditions, the pastor is often expected to teach the confirmation class, even if that is the only teaching expected of the pastor. Among Presbyterians, the "pastor's class" of the nineteenth century was a "response to perceived failings and/or excesses of the Sunday School."[8] Likewise, today pastors who are realistic know that they cannot expect twelve- or thirteen-year-old confirmands to bring much knowledge or significant experience of Christian faith to the class. This is as much evidence as anyone should need to be convinced that educational programs in most congregations are not effective. This ineffectiveness is so common that confirmation curriculum is now written as an *introduction* to Christian faith.

Christian educators and pastors recognize that there is a crisis in confirmation practices. Yet, instead of asking how teens can be guided toward a commitment of life to Jesus Christ, most rearrange the content of a short intense period of study about Christian faith. The issue is not the content of the class. The issue is how a congregation can provide significant spiritual formation over an extended period of time that will prepare young women and men to decide whether they are ready to make the commitment of a lifetime.

It is not possible to know what it means to confess faith in Jesus Christ as Lord until at least the teen years. Before that, children who have been baptized are considered Christian because they participate in the life of a Christian congregation. A confession of faith should be the most important decision of a lifetime. It is a choice that gives meaning to all other commitments. This choice can be made only by someone who knows that there are alternatives.

Movement toward a confession of faith in Jesus Christ can begin in childhood through the formative experience of weekly worship. In congregations where children study while adults worship, the spiritual loss is immeasurable. Teens who appreciate worship are usually people who learned to love the Word, spoken and sung, when they were children. This habit of worship is most easily learned in childhood as children learn the language and rituals of faith. The meaning of worship can take on new importance in the teen years, especially as they become aware of why they worship.

Even though "the family pew" has changed dramatically, when teens attend a confirmation class as preparation for joining a church, they may be only affirming loyalty to the ideals of "the family pew." If parents present their children for baptism because it is a family ritual, the same parents probably will want their children to formally join the church because it is a family tradition.

If members of a confirmation class join church and then "drop out," it is because present practice only ritualizes their right to decide whether they will go to church or not. The decision to join the church can be that of loyalty to a Christian way of life. When it is less than this, confirmation rituals are a mockery of the spiritual capacity and hunger of teens to find a way of life that is an alternative to the nihilistic ways of "the world."

The idolatry of "the family pew" may be the motivating force for such decisions if the life of a congregation is organized around rituals that do not give meaning to the lives of participants. "Traditional" rituals, moral and social values, may "work" in parts of the country where a Protestant ethos is still a part of regional culture. But where the rituals that are most important are those associated with the family life cycle—marriage, baptism, and burial—the rituals are only rites of passage for "birthright" Christians who "prefer to grow their own" new members.

Under these circumstances, when adults join a church after attending a few semioptional new member classes, there is no reason to expect their commitment to be any more than that of teen communicants. With the exception of adult converts, the attitudes of adults about church membership are often the same as the level of commitment expected of them when they confirmed their baptism.

*Spiritual Integrity in Membership Rituals*

The teen years are the optimal time to learn what makes Christians different from other people. During the early teen years, young people have a growing capacity to reflect about God, life's meaning, and life's commitments. Critical judgment about pastors, parents, teachers, and youth leaders are natural to them. But they are also ready to fall in love. They are attracted to adults who are enthusiastic and committed Christians. They need to know adults who are comfortable enough with their own sexuality to be able to discuss the sexual issues of youth today with candor and honesty.

The ministry of all Christians—service to God in family, in the church, and in the world—is a commitment attractive to teens looking for a life worth living. The natural idealism of youth can be nurtured through study, worship, service, and fellowship with adults they trust and like. Since these are the years when teens need to distinguish themselves from their parents, it is especially important that they begin to transfer affections to other "mothers," "fathers," "brothers," and "sisters" who can help guide them into the larger household of faith.

Teens' readiness for commitment to love and work for the well-being of others makes them especially critical of anything done only because it is "the tradition." They are unusually sensitive to the shallowness of adults who lack depth of commitment or ability to articulate their own faith persuasively. Teens are ready to choose Christian faith if they are offered a discipline worth following and work worthy of their best effort by adults who model faithful ministry to them.

This would be much more powerfully ritualized if teens were responsible for choosing baptism as their response in faith to the reality of the new life in Christ they have experienced. In the present cultural context, they may be the age group most likely to appreciate the relief of leaving the pressures and values of the old life behind.

*Confirmation as Baptismal Candidacy*

The spiritual formation practices of the church before the Constantinian era suggest an alternative for today. Early church documents indicate that young adults and adults seeking knowledge of God and considering baptism into Christian fellowship belonged to a group known as the catechumens. The major educational effort of the church was invested in providing three years of instruction and carefully guided participation in worship and service to prepare catechumens for baptismal candidacy. This process was designed to immerse catechumens in Scripture and to provide teachers who were exemplary Christians to guide them in their decision about baptism. The candidate and the church both participated in deciding whether the catechumen was ready to make a lifelong commitment to God.

Catechetical instruction included the exposition of the Golden Rule and the two great commandments, love of God and love of neighbor. During the period of instruction, catechumens were expected to worship regularly and were permitted to participate in agape meals. They were probably excluded from the Lord's Supper.[9]

It is possible to engage teens in a three-year preparation for church membership while they participate in the worship and work of a congregation. Some congregations already have a three-year period of preparation. All activities in which teens participate are considered part of their preparation. From this more holistic perspective on spiritual formation, this period of training is expected to prepare teens to choose whether they are ready to confess faith in Jesus Christ. If baptism means membership in the Church universal, it may more properly belong to that time in life when a profession of faith in Jesus Christ is possible.

If intentional spiritual formation precedes commitment, it is *only* the ritual and *not* the nature of participation in the congregation that would change. Perhaps choosing the sacrament of baptism rather than a confirmation of infant baptism would distinguish a commitment to Jesus Christ from a choice to join a church. A recent study of factors in effective Christian education found that two denominations—the Southern Baptist Convention and the Disciples of Christ—do not experience a decline in the commitment of teens in the church. They are the only denominations of six included in the study that do not practice infant baptism.[10]

In evangelical and Pentecostal churches, teens do choose their own baptism, usually between the ages of twelve and fifteen. This choice is not the result of intentional spiritual formation, but the effect is similar. Their baptism is more a calling, because they are immersed in the ethos of a congregation. They experience spiritual formation through regular participation in the life of a congregation over an extended period of time. These youths are not motivated primarily by family loyalty. Rather, they choose to commit themselves to live the Christian life as they have learned it from a congregation.

There is resistance among pastors and educators to alternatives to the confirmation class because it sounds like a longer period of preparation. They say that teens will drop out before they are confirmed. The alternatives proposed are *not* longer. They represent a different understanding of preparation with a different objective.

The issue is the nature of the choice being made and how anyone reaches a point of readiness to confess faith in Jesus Christ. Confirmation class is not a time when teens are prepared to be officially confirmed *by* the church. Already baptized teens are being prepared to confirm that Jesus Christ is the Lord of their lives. Baptism is an act of the church through which God's grace is made available. Confirmation is the response of an individual to the reality of God's grace, through which faith is gratefully acknowledged and publicly claimed.

Most current membership rituals communicate a message that belonging to a church is not a serious, life-changing commitment. Congregations perpetuate the illusion that membership in a congregation is the same as confessing faith in Jesus Christ when they refuse to consider alternatives. Especially in a time of membership decline, pastors fear that prospective members might be alienated if a congregation has stated expectations of members.

One of the reasons that congregations grow is that they are clear about what membership represents. The real issue is not whether there are membership requirements in a congregation; it is whether fulfilling the requirements will elicit loyalty to Jesus Christ that is stronger than loyalty to family ideals.

# CHAPTER 8

# Spiritual Formation Through Family Ministries

W hen people live together, all are affected by change in the life of one member. Each is affected in a different way. Events at work or school, children leaving home, new interests of one family member, or any change in social relationships will affect family relationships. A life transition like a family move, marriage or divorce, or any event that seems like a "new life" is a time when growth can occur, but it can also be a time of regression. Each member will respond to change in a different way, but the balance of relationships in the "family" will be disturbed.

Good relationships with parents, children, siblings, or life partners are of great importance to most church members. Yet, in many congregations, these issues are treated as private or peripheral to the life of faith. Opportunities for deepening faith are lost if members can not bring the joys, tragedies, and ethical ambiguities of family life into their church life. A life transition is a time when people are unusually vulnerable, a time when they can learn to see and trust the power of God's grace in their lives in some new way.

In a middle-class Victorian home, each age group had its own room or wing of the house. Many churches look that way, with rooms for children, teens, the choir, and a ladies' parlor. There is usually no place for family groups to learn together and often no place for the men of the congregation. The design of such a church building will influence program planning. Most gatherings are planned for people who are alike in age and marital status. Ironically, a "fellowship hall" presumably intended for mixed gatherings is often a room so large and barren that it discourages fellowship altogether.

When normal life events like teen-parent alienation, marital stress, mid-life crises, and decisions about elderly parents are hidden behind superficial relationships in a congregation, conversations that will encourage families to minister to one another are not likely to happen. It is a travesty of the nature of the church if the programs of a congregation encourage members to pretend that their family has no trouble or tensions. If members are to learn faithful living from one another, they have to know and trust others enough to confide in one another.

### Pastoral Care as the Ministry of All Christians

The idolatries of "the family pew" are quietly killing the spirit of Christian faith. A church program with Victorian origins and objectives has little relevance to lives lived in the late-twentieth century. In congregations where one pastor is responsible for preaching, worship, family-related rituals, all pastoral care, and administration, that pastor is doing a disproportionate amount of the work of the church.

Pastors who best fulfill congregational desires for a family chaplain will be least able to grow spiritually through participation in their own families. Every Christian is called to do some of the work of the church. When this does not or cannot happen, the body is bound to be disjointed, even spiritually deformed.

Christian spiritual formation optimally involves lifelong participation in a Christian fellowship where members can learn and practice faithful response to God. The provision of a context in which people can come to appreciate the Lordship of Jesus Christ does not require a major reorganization of a congregation. It does require an evaluation of the extent to which present activities contribute to positive spiritual formation for all age groups in the church. It will probably require thinking about different objectives for existing groups. It will probably mean forming some new groups to give explicit attention to learning through family-related ministries.

It is well known among pastors that many members want only the pastor to call on them when they are in need of pastoral care. But why does *pastoral care* so often mean care given *only* by pastors? Why doesn't it mean the care that all Christians are to give to one another?

If the pastor is the "paid" caller who represents the church, it deprives others of an opportunity for growth through ministry. When the pastor does all of the calling, members never know the blessing that comes from being with one another, of learning from one another in times of trouble, of praying with and for one another.

Many people believe that pastors are trained to give specialized pastoral care. In some cases this is correct. On the other hand, members of a congregation may credit a pastor with far more specialized knowledge than is really the case. Many pastors have very little formal training that would prepare them to respond adequately to the very complicated kinds of issues members may bring to them.

The mystique surrounding pastoral care is another example of dualistic thinking about the church and ministry. When only men were ordained, the pastor's wife often made calls at the homes of church members. Since there is more equality in ordination, the pastor's spouse is not as likely to function as an unpaid pastoral assistant. But the idea that the minister is better equipped than anyone else to make home and hospital calls persists because the work of pastoral care has been spiritualized.

The association of family trouble or divorce with the end of a life may imply that an ordained person is more spiritually qualified to be able to help. That may be so, but it does not have to mean that no one else in the congregation is spiritually qualified to engage in pastoral care.

Pastoral care literature is sometimes written as if people suffering from disappointment in some family relationship need a pastor to lead them through a grief process. In fact, parents can feel that a child who refuses to conform to their way of life is dead. But this way of thinking about the normal patterns and tensions of family life makes it seems like the evils of "the world" have invaded "the Christian home."

Calling in the pastor, then, is something like calling in the tribal shaman to drive away evil spirits. This attitude about the normal life experiences of Christians implicitly denies that new life is always available through participation in a congregation. Probably the area in which members of a congregation can be most helpful in caring for one another is related to the ministry of parenthood.

A pastor can train and supervise lay ministers in virtually every aspect of pastoral care. There are crisis situations where the pastor is expected to have the specialized skill and experience needed. But it is legitimate for the pastor to facilitate home calls and pastoral care by involving members of a congregation who have gifts in pastoral care.

In addition to equipping laity for counseling and calling on members, the pastor can teach members to recognize the capacity of every member for pastoral care. With active encouragement from the pastor, members of the congregation can and should minister to one another out of their own experience with times of transition in family life, work-related issues, illness, and death. This kind of mutual ministry occurs naturally in every congregation between people who are already friends. But they may think of this only as an act of friendship without realizing that all acts of compassion are ministry in the name of Jesus Christ.[1]

*Vocational Guidance as Pastoral Care*

Every family can expect to have times of stress when they will need help from other Christians. Those times are so predictable that some congregations have ongoing support groups which members attend when a particular need arises. These groups are issue-oriented and function like a drop-in center. Long-term membership is not expected.

In smaller congregations, people who have already been through some family-related trauma or who have experienced recent bereavement can be encouraged to minister to others in similar situations. These are times when members of a congregation will be more gifted or better prepared than the pastor to give spiritual direction to one another through mutual ministry.

Spiritualizing the nature of pastoral care limits the range of problems considered spiritual enough to merit serious attention. Vocational guidance is not usually treated as a pastoral-care issue, but there is growing recognition that what happens at work deeply affects the lives of church members. It affects their church relationships, and it affects their family life.

Work-related support groups are usually crisis-oriented. Some congregations have groups for people—usually men— who are out of work. But men, women, and teens all need help in reflecting about their expectations of work or career. It would come as relief to many to realize that Christians do not have to regard work as satisfying or as fulfilling. Rather, they can learn to see their work in the world as service to God and an opportunity to witness to their faith.

A life obsessed with personal ambition or level of income leaves no room for ministry in the workplace. Church members need opportunities to discuss how they can live their faith where they work. Cultural attitudes about work, especially expectations of achievement, have considerable bearing on the way church members think about the stewardship of life and income in the congregation.

Christian attitudes about work have different meanings for people in different circumstances. There is now an increasingly large group of unemployed women who are former homemakers. Many have been divorced or widowed and are single parents. Many of them lack self-confidence in their ability to gain employment. Cultural stereotypes about the work world of men can affect both women and men in negative ways. In general, however, men attach too much significance to work performance and recognition of their achievement, while women doubt their ability to function in the public work world.

The way many Christians think about work perpetuates unconscious double standards that affect a wide variety of issues related to work in the world and work in the church. Ordination has been spiritualized if ministry in a congregation is considered the only, or the highest, form of Christian vocation. Every Christian has a full-time Christian vocation, not just pastors.

Members will continue to act as if only pastors have been called to a Christian vocation if pastors do not engage them in an examination of the expectations that control their lives. Pastors will continue to resent the amount of work they are doing "for" the congregation if they do not examine their own attitudes about the work of full-time ministry. Some pastors point out that they are the last generalists left among the professions. This may indicate that a pastor likes to believe that he or she can do it all alone.

Everyone learns how to seek the well-being of others by acting on good intentions. It is more important for the spiritual well-being of a congregation that a pastor facilitate mutual ministry than that the pastor became a specialist in pastoral care. When members are involved in caring for others, a foundation has been laid for reflection about *all* work as Christian vocation. If members experience service to others in the congregation as *their* ministry, it is much easier for them to see that their work in the world is also service to God.

## Family-related Growth Groups

Jesus tells his followers to "love one another" as he loves them. He also tells them to love their neighbor. There is no indication that Jesus regarded some people as less worthy or less in need of love. Instructions to love your neighbor do not locate the neighbor in any particular place. The neighbor of a Christian is any human being, not just a church member or another Christian. The nearest neighbors are those in close physical proximity. For most people, that will mean family members. For many, it also means co-workers in whose presence much of life is lived.

Faithful family membership is the only ministry held in common by all Christians. Almost everyone has mother, father, brother, sister, husband, wife, or child. When *family* is defined as nearest neighbor, this can also include any two people who live together.

Recent statistics about divorce and violence in the home are a fair indication that it is very difficult to really love the nearest neighbor. There is no family relationship that is not subject to feelings of anger, hostility, or even hatred. No family relationship is immune to feelings of alienation.

Most of the family problems pastors hear about are related to a temporary time of stress during which members seek counsel. The most common issues are marital strain, parent-child alienation, and worry about responsibility for aging parents. These are all issues worthy of theological reflection with a group. Church members who bring their problems to the pastor may not realize how many other members in the congregation have had or are having similar experiences. This is especially true where local convention requires keeping up appearances of family harmony.

Many family-related problems can be referred to growth groups organized so church members with similar experience can minister to one another. Every individual has to respond to his or her unique situation. But members are denied access to the spiritual resources of the Christian community if there are no groups where they can get perspective on their issue, where they can pray with and for one another. People no longer feel so terribly alone when they can discuss their feelings and their faith with one another.

There are many ways in which church members can and do reach out to one another in time of trouble: visitation, providing food when there is illness or death, or informally commiserating with one another. But social conventions that keep people from admitting that they are suffering some family-related grief prevent Christians from being able to give God's love to others in times when they should be able to rely on the Christian community.

The power of these unwritten rules about social life should not be underestimated. A study of congregations with effective Christian education programs suggests there is strong evidence that congregations consisting of adults who do not rely on one another cannot adequately minister to one another.

Many adults don't experience a sense of well-being, security or peace in their faith. They have trouble seeking spiritual growth through study, reflection, prayer and discussion with others. And they do little to serve others through acts of "love and justice."[2]

The study also indicates that when adults experience a sense of personal well-being, they have been helped to integrate faith with life and to see work, family, social relationships, and political choices as part of religious life.

If the life of a congregation revolves around the one-to-one relationships between pastor and people, the corporate nature of the Christian community is obscured. A congregation cannot be the people of God working together to build up the Body of Christ if people lack opportunities to serve one another in love. If the trend of individualism in the services given by pastors to members of the congregation is not reversed, church members will not know themselves as persons with gifts for ministry. If members do not learn what it means to belong to "the Body of Christ" through service to one another, they will have little inclination to see or believe that the church is called to serve the world.

A spiritual growth group is a learning opportunity for individuals who are experiencing a time of unusual stress.[3] The pastor or lay leader with gifts for guiding a particular group should be the organizer and initial leader of the group. Once the pastor or original leader establishes patterns for a growth group around an issue that affects the lives of a number of members, the group can continue with a revolving membership and leadership shared by members.

In one congregation, a group for the middle-aged "children" of aging parents continued for a four-year period with constantly changing membership led by members with small-group skills. As members became comfortable with a format of reflection guided by Scripture and prayer and the needs of members, they took turns leading the group.

A family-issue growth group helps individuals cope with their particular situation. But it is more than just a coping device. They can grow spiritually if they are able to sympathize with and learn from one another. They can grow as they learn to receive help from others. A growth group is a setting where people can learn that traditional spiritual disciplines lend perspective and reassurance when life is confusing and difficult. In this setting, they are motivated to learn to read the Bible as a source of perspective, correction, and encouragement as they participate in a group. This kind of spiritual discipline can train Christians how to rely on God's grace even when faith would otherwise seem impossible.

When any ongoing group—like the "Children of Aging Parents" group—is listed regularly on the church calendar, the group will become a tradition, albeit a new one. A growth group offers spiritual formation for adults who might otherwise seek counseling or simply resort to stoic resignation when troubled. Where there is an ongoing group available to help members respond to particular family issues, the new tradition gives spiritual-formation opportunities to more adults than is usual in many congregations.

Family-related growth groups engage adults in life-changing spiritual formation because this experience can change attitudes about family life. Over time, the availability of family-related growth groups will make it acceptable to confide in and learn from others in the Christian community.

Congregations that give priority to family-related issues of members are often known for their spiritual vitality. Family-related growth groups sometimes attract new members, especially people who would not seek out pastoral care. In a culture where people are desperate to find satisfying personal relationships, a congregation can be a light shining in the wilderness of modern family life.

*Growth Groups for Parents*

There are many congregations in which the only attention given to parents has been related to Sunday School. Instead of asking how the church can assist adults in their calling as Christian parents, attempts are made to enlist them as supporters of the Sunday School. This does not ask about the spiritual well-being of parents. It may very well assume it.

Growth groups for parents can be offered as part of adult education in a congregation. In a small congregation, groups can be organized on an *ad hoc* basis in response to particular needs of members; in larger congregations, the size of the congregation may warrant ongoing groups that parents can join on a short-term basis. The times of special need for parents are usually the times of transition as their children grow older.

For instance, new parents need help adjusting to the way their marriage is changed by becoming parents. Parents of preschool children sometimes ask for help understanding the religious development of children; they want to know how to talk about God with their children. Parents of school-age children need help understanding how to deal with the non-Christian values and attitudes their children learn at school and through the media. Parents in mixed marriages ask for help regarding the religious education of their children.

From the late middle-school years until the time when a "child" leaves home, Christian parents need a place where they can meet other adults who share their life values. Many parents are aware that their children will be pressured to experiment with sex, drugs, and/or alcohol during the teen years. Parents need help in adjusting relationships and family rules as children grow older so they can experience the freedom and the responsibility they need in order to grow up.[4] In some congregations, this kind of learning and support occurs in parent-education groups.[5]

Optimal spiritual formation for the children of the church requires consistency in the attitudes and values communicated at church and at home. Parents need the church to take the initiative in helping them to be self-conscious about the way Christian values and attitudes are related to family relationships. They need instruction about Christian perspectives on all of life, as well as opportunities to reflect about family-related issues. Members may need more basic instruction about Christian attitudes and values than pastors imagine. These needs should be regularly addressed in sermons, in Bible study groups, as well as in parent-education groups.

The modern Protestant tendency to believe that children

should be like their parents makes it unusually difficult to adjust to differences between generations that are due primarily to a major economic and cultural transition. Some child-rearing literature gives the impression that parental "mistakes" during early childhood can "cause" irreversible flaws in the personalities of their children. There is a common impression that something must have gone wrong in the mother-child relationship if a young man or a young woman is not "normal" according to the criteria of "the family pew."

A Christian view of the parental role offers freedom from the psychological determinism of child-rearing literature that assigns God-like powers to parental influence. The formative influence of family life and the personal example of parents is an important element in the lives of all children. Yet, there is considerable mystery in the way any personality is formed through various cultural experiences that include church, schools, and media, as well as family. Parents can play a powerful role in shaping the emotional responses of children during the early childhood years. Yet, this influence forms only the rudiments of the human spirit. A growth group for parents should be a place where parents can acquire a balanced sense of the limits of their influence as parents, as well as support for their responsibility of servant ministry at home.

The aspect of Christian spiritual formation that is likely to be most difficult for parents and pastors is the inclusion of sexuality education in the spiritual formation of children and teens. A spirit-flesh dualism is the unconscious governing principle in any congregation where leaders do not consider education about sexuality a high priority for all ages in the church. Pastors and parents are the people most likely to think about the sexual behavior of children and youth. Neither can offer spiritual formation in this area unless they are aware of the way new sexual self-consciousness affects the lives of teens.

The ability to communicate about delicate issues with teenage "children" comes through an ease of interpersonal exchange that is established by parents when their children are quite young. Healthy self-respect and respect for others is the best protection a parent can give a child against undesirable or premature sexual experimentation. Respect and care for the sexuality of children in the family is not achieved by parental lectures when erotic desire suddenly becomes obvious in the early teen years. Children who learn self-respect at home have been blessed with a family in which respect for others is built into the web of family relationships.

Parents who are comfortable with their own sexuality—and with each other—can more casually discuss the expression of sexuality and its pleasures and perils with their children. These parents can be trusted not to laugh at what may seem like a silly question. Their children know that their parents are available for conversation but are not likely to press their opinions on them. This capacity for treating the sexual identity of children as crucial to spiritual formation is one of the best gifts a Christian parent can give to a child growing up in a world incapable of respecting sexuality. This gift is especially valuable when a parent is aware that a child may have a homosexual orientation.

Members of the early Christian churches frequently gathered in homes, possibly daily, for worship. The writer of Ephesians urges consultation among members to discern what kind of self-sacrificing love is "pleasing to the Lord." Christian parents today have a similar need to discern and to learn from each other what is good, right, and true concerning the daily life of Christians. It is not likely that Christians in families can live together in Christ if family members have not participated in and learned the meaning of repentance and forgiveness through their life as members of a Christian community.

One of the best ways a congregation can support two-parent families is to give adequate attention to marriage from a Christian perspective. Many tensions in marital relationships can be resolved by helping a couple distinguish reality from overly romantic expectations about family life. The marital relationships of church members can be examined, clarified, and strengthened through study and reflection about Christian views of marriage.

A family is a system where children form their earliest impressions about relationships and themselves. Attitudes about sexuality, ways of expressing affection, and rules about personal relationships are all learned at home to some extent. For this reason, more attention to the marital relationship of parents can directly benefit their children.

Depending on the makeup of membership in a congregation, growth groups for parents might include all parents, whether they are married or single, in one group. However, life in a single-parent household differs significantly from that in a two-parent household. This is especially true when the parent is a woman with financial problems, which is often the case. If at all possible, a congregation should consider a special ministry to support single parents.

All ministry of Christians to one another in the congregation can be training for service at home, at work, and at play. Growth groups to support parents in servant ministry at home might be considered essential spiritual formation for adults. There may be no other set of human beings so in need of reassurance about the love of God in the modern world.

## The Family-cluster House-church

A "family-cluster house-church" can support the family ministry of parents through an ongoing relationship of several family groups. A pastor usually helps form this kind of family growth group, finds program resources, and gives oversight. Since a house-church works on the principle that parents accept responsibility for leadership, the pastor should not be the leader and need not be directly involved in meetings of the group.[6]

The family-cluster house-church is one of the most promising spiritual growth groups available to support Christian parents in the nurture and instruction of their own children. Resources for intergenerational Bible study in groups including children, teens, and adults can be prepared by adapting curriculum written for children. It is often easier to use Bible commentaries to adapt material intended for children for use with teens and adults than to adapt adult curriculum for use with children. Intergenerational curriculum is published from time to time, but availability is sporadic.

A typical house-church consists of three or four families who covenant to meet together regularly in homes for a minimum of three months. The combination of meeting as the extended church family to share meals, study, and fellowship together is a powerful aid to spiritual discipline and communication in family life. The easiest time to establish family-unit commitment to intergenerational education is when children are beginning elementary school.

Habits of Bible study and prayer can be learned quite naturally by children when they are just learning to read. They learn Bible stories, biblical language, and religious ritual most naturally during the early elementary-school years, for these are the golden years for memorization. This is a time when children are highly motivated to do what they see and hear parents and adults in the congregation doing.

In a house-church format for Bible study and prayer, three age groups can learn the same content, but each group learns differently. Children are not capable of theological reflection about the meaning of stories, because all theological language is abstract. Because they can think only about concrete reality, children can be expected to identify emotionally with people in stories.

Teens are the group most naturally capable of entertaining a variety of meanings. If encouraged to raise questions about how a passage is to be understood, they can stimulate adults who may believe that they already know what a passage is about to reconsider the meaning.

Intergenerational Bible study has an added advantage in that no prior knowledge about the content of the Bible is presupposed. Since children are learning stories for the first time, this is an ideal setting for adults who have never learned basic Bible content.

A typical house-church format includes a commitment to meet for a minimum of two hours at least twice a month. Most groups find that if they do not agree on a day and a time at the outset, attendance is irregular. Usually a meal is shared and then at least a full hour is devoted to study and informal worship. Responsibility for the meal is shared by all members.

Leadership for each meeting can be rotated between family groups, or shared by several adult and teen members who have skills in leading Bible study. Planning can be done like Sunday

School curriculum, in three-month units by topic. Members with the best Bible study skills probably should be designated as the coordinators to organize topics, resources, leaders, and meeting places for three months at a time.

Food, feeding, and nourishment in corporate gatherings are focal symbols of well-being and wholeness in the Christian tradition. Corporate gatherings for meals have been part of Christian faith since the earliest gatherings of Christians. Daily fellowship around the table is essential for good communication in any family. Yet, the eating habits, cooking habits, and the ways families communicate have changed over the last twenty years. It may be that the church will have to encourage parents to recognize the importance of table fellowship for families. A house-church gathering is a place where family members can learn the value of communal meals.

In a house-church, the shared meal and table fellowship is as important as the study of Scripture. People from families where members do not see one another or communicate regularly cannot be expected to know much about intimacy in relation-ships. Genuine knowledge of self and other persons grows through thoughtful, attentive communication on a daily basis over a long period of time.

The love of Christians for one another can be experienced when members of several families break bread together on a regular basis around the table of their extended church family. A house-church gathering can be a learning lab for Christian family life. It also can be an experience of intimate friendship that lays foundations for deeper appreciation of expressions of God's love through the sacraments.

Members of a congregation where people are strangers to one another find it difficult to imagine or even comprehend the meanings associated with fellowship at the Table of the Lord. Members of a community of strangers are not very likely to experience themselves as part of the communion of saints. It is important to the life of a congregation that parents learn the relational skills needed for good communication and respect among members of a family. Then family imagery used to express God's love in liturgy can have positive life-giving connotations.

### House-church as an Extended Family for Youths

Youths have a special need for positive experiences with a family where members care about one another. There are young people who are church members but do not come from a church family. There are other young people who long for a better family. They may live in a disorganized family. They may be victims of sexual abuse. They may suffer from a strained relationship between their parents. Family clusters can give young people a different and sometimes better experience of what it means to belong to a family.

To facilitate this kind of ministry to youth, a pastor might ask several families in which the parent or parents are especially gifted in relating to youths to form a cluster that can include several young people with the family groups. This kind of intergenerational experience often attracts young people who will not attend other youth-oriented activities. This experience can give them a "family" in the church. It also can give them more positive role models for marriage and family life than they are likely to experience elsewhere.

Teens from disorganized families can sometimes be identified by their behavior. They act out more than their peers and usually demand excessive amounts of attention from the pastor or youth leader. On the other hand, there are "sad" teens who feel so different because of trouble at home that they may be very quiet, or simply refuse to participate in youth programs at church. An exploration of why young people are inactive can be a way of learning more about some of the family-related needs of members.

The family-cluster house-church has been used in some small congregations instead of Sunday School as the basic form of education for children and youth. When a group of parents in a community of faith work together to educate their children in the life of faith, this gives members of each family something in common with other families. When members of one family share the same learning experience each week, they have an ongoing topic of conversation between house-church meetings. When this happens, children learn about Christian family life as part of their experience of belonging to a community of Christians.

Effectiveness of a family-cluster house-church depends on the capacity and willingness of parents to learn with and teach their own children. In a congregation too small for a Sunday school that offers classes for all age groups, this might be considered one alternative. In a congregation where the leadership is available to offer a variety of learning opportunities for people of all ages, the inclusion of a family-cluster house-church is ideal for a broad approach to the spiritual formation of family members.

*Intergenerational Study Groups*

Many congregations cannot find enough volunteers to maintain even minimal education programs. Traditional ways of segregating age groups from one another can lead pastors or Christian education committees to overlook some viable alternatives to traditional ways of organizing educational ministries.

If a congregation is to work together for the mutual edification of all members, regardless of age, sex, or marital status, every member can benefit from learning experiences that include persons from two or more age groups. Where worship or education programs systematically separate children, young people, adults, and older adults from one another, no one can benefit from the natural spiritual strengths of other age groups. For instance, some single adults want to know the children and youth of a congregation but have no opportunity. They may want to participate in activities with couples or family groups but find themselves excluded by the way programs and activities are organized.

Older adults are sometimes attuned to the lives of children and youth in a congregation in ways that parents are not. Some older adults who miss seeing their own grandchildren are delighted for opportunities to befriend some of the children in their congregation. They often have no way to express this if they belong to a congregation where the only place they ever see children is during the children's sermon. Older adults and single adults are often overlooked as candidates for leadership in ministry with children in the congregation.

A family-cluster house-church appeals primarily to adults who are already committed Christians and to families in which the parents are eager for an extended family experience. A less demanding form of intergenerational learning can be arranged by adding an intergenerational Bible study class to the Sunday School. For instance, an intergenerational Sunday School class that mixes youths with adults can foster learning in which the independent thinking and questioning necessary to choosing Christian faith as a way of life is encouraged. Since it is natural for teens to question all that is traditional, this mix gives all members an opportunity to examine their faith commitments.

It is not unusual anymore to find that only one or two members of a family unit are members of a congregation. Increasingly, people from different kinds of families are attracted to the life of a congregation because of the quality of relationships they experience there.

Members of a congregation are able to support one another in time of need because the family situations of each is different. It is because members of a congregation are free from the dynamics of daily family life together that they *can* be a source of spiritual strength, solace, and inspiration to others. When one is weak, another is strong (I Cor. 12:14-26).

A pastor is different from other members of a congregation in several respects. As the designated leader of a congregation, the pastor is expected to interpret the meaning of the Christian life. That means that the pastor can influence the way the people of God think about the church, ministry, their families, and all of life.

As the spiritual director of the life of the congregation, the pastor is the person charged with oversight of all church-related programs. A knowledge of the way dualistic attitudes lead laity to believe that only pastors are called to full-time ministry can be freeing to any pastor who is doing too much of the work of the church. Insight into the way members think about the work of the church can be a first step toward freeing the whole people of God from bondage to a dysfunctional division of labor that makes it difficult for all to claim their God-given gifts for ministry.

# CHAPTER 9

# *"The Family Pew" Revisited:*
## The Church as the Household of God

The structure of thought in Western culture differs from that of Eastern cultures. It is typical of Western cultures, especially in the nineteenth century, to think in terms of dualism and linear development, of change as progress or regress. During the nineteenth century, these tendencies dominated theological responses to changing demographics and the rise of nations as centers of power. In Europe, Søren Kierkegaard wrote books like *Stages Along Life's Way* as a response to the philosophical idealism of his day. In the philosophy of men like G.W.F. Hegel, Kierkegaard saw theories about stages of human consciousness and progress in world history that he thought could lead Christians away from reliance on Scripture as a source of truth about human life.

In *Stages,* Kierkegaard described three related but distinct sets of attitudes about life which are typical of ways that people relate to God, self, and others. He hoped to demonstrate the fallacy of imagining that the well-being of human life does not finally depend on faith in Jesus Christ. Kierkegaard's stages are intended to describe ways of experiencing life that are typical of cultures, as well as "stages" of consciousness an individual could pass through on the way to faith in Jesus Christ. Although every generation in the church inherits a religious tradition, each generation must learn faith anew if it is to be genuine faith in Jesus Christ.

Hegel's type of idealism had great influence on the formal discipline of Christian education, which has been in existence for less than a century. In the United States, pioneers like George A. Coe were caught up in the linear, progressive educational theories of John Dewey and enthusiasm for "a Christian America." The earliest theories in Christian education, at the beginning of the twentieth century, often equated good Christians with good citizens.

### Faith Development Theory and the Nuclear Family

During the last twenty years, changes in family life and in church demographics have rekindled interest in Christian nurture and in new progressive theories about human nature. Conservatives have rediscovered Horace Bushnell's *Christian Nurture*. Conservatives and liberals alike have debated the use of faith-development theory in Christian education.[1]

While professional educators and theorists debate the merits of the theory, others have been quick to assimilate it into the work of Christian education in a congregation. The uncritical assimilation of faith-development theory into educational ministry may very well have been more influential in the lives of congregations than the debates that professionals have among themselves. For instance, in the recent three-and-a-half-year study of effective Christian education, the research was conceptualized in terms of an assumption that "maturity in faith" can be defined as integrated faith. Judgments were made that assumed a distinction between persons who demonstrated "mature" faith and those who did not.[2]

In a time when changing membership patterns and changing family life made it obvious that children do not necessarily inherit the faith of their parents, the time was ripe for receptivity to developmental theories about faith. Those theories are reassuring to people who suspect that "traditional" values are being eroded by life in a technological, secular society. The assumption that there are discernible patterns of human development conveys the idea that if parents or schools or churches transmit their values at *the right time* in the developmental cycle they can have some confidence that their way of life will be reproduced in the lives of the children.

Professors and researchers in Christian education have created faith-development theory by applying the psychosocial theories of Erik Erikson, the cognitive-development theories of Jean Piaget, and the moral-development theories of Lawrence Kohlberg to the life of faith. However, a preoccupation with the "development" of faith can lead people primarily to ask *how* faith is transmitted. This is basically the same project as that of Horace Bushnell. When the subject of Christian education is how faith develops or is transmitted, the equally important task of theological reflection about the content of faith may be neglected.

Popular applications of theories about stages of faith can give the impression that there is a developmental sequence, through which most children and youths in the church can or do pass ,on the way to becoming adult Christians. For those who miss some of the theoretical subtleties, faith appears to "develop" as naturally as bodies can be expected to grow. This approach shifts the focus of educational ministries away from what God is doing through the church to almost total preoccupation with what teachers and parents can do to assure themselves that their children will have faith.

> For by grace you have been saved through faith, and this is not your own doing; it is the gift of God—not the result of works, so that no one may boast. For we are what he [sic] has made us, created in Christ Jesus for good works, which God prepared beforehand to be our way of life. (Eph. 2:8-10)

It is difficult to translate the biblical view that faith brings together the eternal love of God and the human longing to be loved into the language of human development. Faith described primarily as a human phenomenon can give the impression that the purpose of education in the church is to lead people through stages of faith. This makes salvation seem like one more human achievement.

This approach to faith formation is the opposite of the traditional assumption that in Jesus Christ salvation has already been accomplished. The objective of traditional spiritual direction is to guide persons into an appreciation of what God is already doing for them.

The purpose of traditional spiritual formation—the language used to describe faith formation before the time of Christian education—is to deepen awareness of what it means to claim and live through faith that is "the gift of God." The life and teachings of Jesus Christ provide the form *and* the content for traditional spiritual formation.

> By themselves the spiritual disciplines can do nothing; they can only get us to the place where something can be done. They are God's means of grace. The inner righteousness we seek is not something that can be poured on our heads. God has ordained the disciplines of the spiritual life as the means by which we are placed so He [sic] can bless us. In this regard it would be proper to speak of "the way of disciplined grace." It is "grace" because it is free: it is "disciplined" because there is something for us to do. Once we clearly understand that God's grace is unearned and unearnable, and if we expect to grow, we must take up a consciously chosen course of action involved in both individual and group life. That is the purpose of the spiritual disciplines.[3]

It is through the experience of acting like followers of Jesus Christ that people come to appreciate what it means to grow up into "the measure of the full stature of Christ" (Eph. 4:13). Throughout the history of Christianity there has been an assumption that faith does have phases, that the quality of faith does change and should deepen. Yet, this is not the same as saying that there are discernible stages through which a person *should* pass if faith is to "mature." New Testament stories of disciples learning to follow the way of Jesus are signposts that can guide all would-be followers of Jesus along the way of "saving" faith. It is possible to acknowledge phases in faith while leaving plenty of room for doubt, questioning, surprise, and the unexpected.

An unfortunate outcome of applied faith-development theory is that it has been used to reinforce or even reintroduce some "family pew" illusions about Christian faith. Writers of family-life literature in the church now advise parents about the way that the faith of children develops in "the Christian home." Despite the fact that there is no longer only one kind of family in most congregations, pictures in some family-life magazines still depict the ideal Christian family—two parents and two children, all smiling.

If such literature implies that children should experience unconditional love in "the Christian home," this misrepresents the role of parents in the faith of their children.

Both Calvin and Luther expected the family to function as "a little church."[4] It seemed reasonable in the sixteenth century that parents could be expected to teach catechism to their children at home and that families would pray together. Recovery of the biblical idea that all Christians are gifted for ministry required attention to the spiritual formation of all Christians, not just those called to priesthood. There has been a tendency ever since to expect "the Christian home" to function as a source of spiritual formation, as the monastery had been the spiritual home for monks and priests.

A preoccupation with faith stages may perpetuate an illusion that spiritual wholeness is a human achievement. An uncritical use of faith-development theory can reduce Christian education to another American scheme for self-fulfillment. It also runs the risk of reintroducing harmful illusions about the power of parents to form the faith of their own children.

The term *nuclear family* is used by sociologists to refer to the smallest family unit, typically that of two parents and their children. In this time of changing family structure, *nuclear* is an ironic choice to designate the smallest set of family relationships. The nuclear family is an isolated family. It is often a family wrenched out of extended family traditions and relationships. It is not unusual to find explosive relationships between members of families isolated from friendship with people like themselves. It is not unusual to find congregations where the emotional volatility of the family life of members is replicated in the life of the congregation.[5]

As is the case with atomic power, the nuclear family has the potential to be a social force that is constructive or destructive. When a congregation has social networks in which intergenerational relationships are possible, parents are relieved of sole responsibility for the faith of their children. When this happens, it is easier to see that the American ideal of a self-sufficient family is not only impossible; it is undesirable.

### The Church as the Family of Faith

Throughout human history, the family has been known to perform a limited number of functions, which vary according to cultural circumstances. The list can include procreation; protection of the young; provision of food, shelter, and clothing; recreation; affection; and basic education. Today, every one of these functions can be carried out by persons other than two parents who are married to each other. This includes reproduction.

Until the industrial revolution of the nineteenth century, children had economic value to their parents; they participated in the work of the family that kept food on the table and clothes on their backs. Since then, children have become an increasing expense at the same time that they no longer contribute to the economic well-being of the family. An outstanding characteristic of the nuclear family since then is the extent to which some parents may be an almost exclusive source of affection for children.[6]

A shift in the role of parents in the lives of children has been under way since early in the nineteenth century. The myth of "the self-sufficient family" comes from a time when farm families no longer had to cooperate with other families to produce life necessities. The "self-sufficient" family today is associated with the economic independence of "respectable" middle-class families in towns and suburbs. Believing that this is the only acceptable type of family for Christians is more possible where men support their families and women can afford the luxury of devoting themselves to being full-time homemakers and mothers.

Change in the family as a social institution in the 1960s came at a time when family relationships were already fragile because of the extent to which parents—or a parent—had become the primary source of affection for children. Even when it is economically possible to look like an "ideal" family, the younger generation may not know or be able to appreciate the expectations their parents have of them.

Christian parents who care about the values of their children are rightly concerned about the moral and social values communicated through the public schools. Public schools inevitably reflect the changing values of the culture. They exist to mediate the political ideals of the nation. Since the Constitution guarantees freedom in the practice of religion, no citizen can expect the public schools to teach religious values. The time is past when Christian parents could count on the public schools to be an agency of the church teaching Christian values.

Given the nature of the changing role of family and school as social institutions, children are now instructed and cared for by a cadre of professionals. Parents spend endless hours taking children to lessons and practice and children's activities—music, dance, sports, Scouts, and other activities. Social historian Christopher Lasch deplores the power now ascribed to people in the mental-health professions. He asserts that parents are forfeiting their most important role in trusting counselors and therapists to grant psychic well-being to their children.[7]

In theory, a family of Christians should be a place where members find the kind of affection that Herbert Anderson describes.

A family of Christian people is sustained by the bonds of affection that transform it into a community of compassion. . . . A family shaped by Christian principles is therefore not only a place of empathy where each one seeks to understand and honor the uniqueness of the other: it is a compassionate community of people who suffer with one another.[8]

This presupposes that adults in the family know Christian principles and are able to live them at home. It also implies that all family members share this commitment.

Most parents of children and teens are so harried between work and keeping up with their children's appointments that they would scarcely recognize themselves described as "a community of compassion." Families in typical congregations find members going off in different directions most days.

For many families, an activity that includes all family members is probably a special event. Members don't have enough in common in many families to be a community of people who "suffer with one another." They may have no idea that other members are suffering. This is one of the reasons that more people attend churches at Christmas, Easter, and possibly Mother's Day. The church does stand as a reminder of what family life might be like.

To some extent, church members do expect the church to support them in faithfulness to family commitments. This is more obvious in congregations where there are support groups for parents and where the pastor communicates the role of the church as the family of faith through careful preparation of all members for baptisms and weddings. This is less obvious where educational programs separate family members by age, sex, or marital status and do not give families of the congregation opportunities to learn faithfulness from one another.

The words translated as *faith* in the New Testament mean both *a belief* and *a way of life*. Christians need to know what they believe in order to live out those beliefs. The children and young people of every congregation need adults who are able to help them think critically about life values to be their teachers, leaders, and role models.

There is an intrinsic connection between a basic education in Christian faith and the love of Christians for one another. The objective of a Christian education is twofold: It is both learning about faith and learning to be faithful. It should guide the learner into personal knowledge of God's love, which is incomplete unless expressed in love of neighbor through ministry. This kind of knowledge is best appropriated through participation in a community of Christians who are self-conscious about their commitment to a Christian way of life. A Christian education that includes study and experience in ministry is more accurately termed *faith formation.*

The word *education* means to lead out or to call out the possibility in the learner. Faith formation involves a kind of education in which the content of learning must be lived to be grasped. The meaning of faith is learned through participation in worship, study, and ministry. When Christians express their learning about faith through ministry, they can learn faithful living from one another.

*Learning Spiritual Discipline*

The values of the American Dream can be destructive habits of thought. People who believe that God's blessing is bestowed on the families of church members have a hard time responding to tragedy. One of the theological issues that troubles Protestants most is the question of why a loving God would allow evil, especially anything "bad" that happens to their family members or friends. The corporate prayers in a congregation are a good indication of the extent to which the concerns of the people are family related. Learning to practice spiritual disciplines cultivates the habit of seeing the world from a wider, more diverse point of view. This is how church members learn to be critical of the social and moral values of the world in which they live and work.[9]

Jesus was very clear that spiritual leaders must be persons whose hearts are instructed and led by a desire to follow his way and his instruction (Matt. 15:8-9). Where a congregation lacks knowledge or experience of following the way of Jesus, people can learn to live the Christian life through study and worship. In the process, they will need guidance to distinguish the values and attitudes of Christians from those of the culture. Otherwise, members can be trapped in repetition of whatever local traditions they associate with what it means to be the church.

The essential ingredients of Christian spiritual formation never change: They are the prayerful study of Scripture and learning to live the life of faith through the influence of other Christians. The way spiritual disciplines are learned does change. There have been times in the history of Christianity when congregations were a learning environment where Christian faith was transmitted from one generation to the next through the depth of commitment of adults in the congregation. There are congregations where this happens today, but they are exceptions.

Members of the Body of Christ can be transformed through their participation in the life of a congregation. This possibility depends, to some extent, on the quality of the life and commitment of members of the congregation. *Transformation,* or *new life in Christ,* refers to the way people are made new by grace through faith in a corporate setting. All Christians, including pastors, are transformed as they try to live the truth they learn about themselves through their relationships with God and neighbor. Hearing eloquent or inspiring sermons does not, by itself, change lives. Lifelong study of Scripture does not, by itself, change lives. Spiritual formation in a congregation requires the leadership of people who understand the challenges of Christians living in a world that is not concerned with Christian values.

In most congregations, spiritual formation will require more intentional creation of an environment in which the life of faith can be learned and lived. Quite possibly, family and work life are the aspects of life in which members are most aware of their personal need for spiritual resources. These are the areas in which people are most vulnerable to misplaced loyalties and loves. It takes more than regular participation in worship to come to appreciate that it is the church, and not blood kin, that is the family of faith.

Christian values can be communicated and reinforced through preaching and worship. But participation in worship is a relatively passive activity. Attitudes and values change when people question their own loyalties, when they recognize that there are competing loyalties in their lives, and when they make informed choices for themselves. In the church, members need opportunities to reflect together about their lives. People are motivated to engage in this kind of reflection by the life issues and experiences that are most real to them. If members of a congregation can begin to see that their work is a way of expressing love to God and neighbor, it could very well transform their way of looking at the world.

## The Spiritual Formation of a Congregation

In every period of church history, the theology of church and ministry is predicated on some canon within *the* canon. In every age, church leaders consciously and unconsciously select biblical stories and themes that fit the needs of their time. For three centuries the canon of "a Christian America" served the needs of a Protestant-dominated culture. In that canon the family was assigned the primary role in socializing children to become the law-abiding, hard-working citizens needed to make the democratic experiment work. From the very beginning of the American experiment with freedom, the churches and ministers have been perceived as providing religious services, without which the experiment could fail. According to the sociology of the American Dream, churches exist to support families so there will be a moral citizenry.

Despite formal separation of church and state, the effect of this arrangement over time has been to covertly control religious leaders by making it appear that the institutions they lead are the bulwark of democracy. From the perspective of this kind of salvation history, both church leaders and churches are of great importance because the American democracy represents God's plan for the world. In some ways, Protestant pastors have been perceived as civil servants.

One of the advantages of living during a cultural transition is that when social roles begin to change, people are in a better position to evaluate how the old social order really worked. In this particular time between the times, older pastors remember when they were called on more often to bless civic functions, when the public schools celebrated only Christmas, and when pastors were expected to join local civic organizations.

Many pastors do not question whether the church exists to serve the nation, or whether America is a Christian nation. They still assume both notions are true. These beliefs have, in the past, robbed most Protestants of their capacity to look at themselves and the nation self-critically. All too often Protestants have retreated into a smug self-righteousness because they have seen themselves as cultural insiders without whom the great American experiment would have failed.

It is common knowledge among some modern church historians that Protestant religion in America has been a civil religion. It is less common to consider the way Protestant civil religion has become a domesticated religion of the white middle-class. Since the nineteenth century, Protestants have been vigilantly defending "the family pew" as the only form of family acceptable to God. They have been far more protective of the sanctity of the family as a social tradition that can never change than they have been of the church. Many have been more willing to question the Bible as a source of truth than they are to question whether the family should be expected to be a source of unconditional love. The consequences of this kind of uncritical allegiance to family love has been a century of church programs designed to insure the future of Christianity through the children of church members.

Every pastor experiences some cultural shock during the early years of service in a congregation. Every congregation is unique, not quite like any other congregation. The life of a congregation is reflected in its history, traditions, language, and belief systems. A new pastor is always an outsider who initially feels like a stranger. It is easier to see the otherness, the uniqueness of a congregation from that perspective.

Pastors can test the extent to which a congregation expects them to function as a civil servant or a family chaplain by evaluating the attitudes of members about marriage and baptism, about educational programs, and about moral issues. The following list is only suggestive. It does not include all possible indications of the formative power of civil religion in the values of a congregation.

- Do members understand why a pastor would refuse to baptize the babies of couples who do not participate in the life of the congregation even though the grandparents are members?

- Does the mother of the bride understand that the pastor directs a wedding ceremony because a Christian marriage is an event in the life of the congregation, not just a family social event?

- How willing are parents of confirmation-age children to support and participate in a lengthy period of preparation for confirmation?

- Do members imagine that a better Sunday School or hiring a youth minister will revitalize the congregation and make it grow?

- If teachers or parents talk about faith development, what do they have in mind? What do they mean by faith?

- What would happen if the pastor said in a sermon that love to neighbor includes loving homosexuals?

- Would the congregation support a ministry to single mothers if that need existed?

- Would the governing board understand if, in deference to the importance of the church year, Memorial Day, Labor Day, Mother's Day, and Father's Day were no longer celebrated?

Even if members have been deeply influenced by the values of civil religion, this does not mean that members don't want the pastor to function as their spiritual leader. But it does mean that they want to hear the good news in a way that conforms with the tradition and canon they inherited. Minds can be changed, and a congregational way of life can be altered when a pastor understands how the traditions of the congregation may limit their ability to experience new life in Christ.

The folkways and loyalties in the life of a congregation change slowly, but there can be new life in a congregation. Just as the ministry of all Christians was rediscovered as an important New Testament motif at the time of the Protestant Reformation, the Bible can always speak some new, liberating word to the need of the people of God. Protestants today need to hear the good news that family life and work life do not have to be the ultimate loyalties of Christians. The people of God need new ways to think about their work commitments and new ways to evaluate their family responsibilities.

In order to address those needs, pastors should be self-conscious about sermon selection and the use of the Bible in preaching. They might ask what social and moral values were communicated through texts preached during the last three years. Are important biblical motifs being overlooked? Do the repeated themes help the people of God evaluate their ordering of loves and loyalties? What is the good news being proclaimed? How does it relate to the reality of life at home and life in the world?

Similar questions can be used to evaluate the purpose and function of all regular church programs.[10] Programs should be evaluated with attention to both form and content. *Form* refers to what programs are available and who they are intended to serve. *Content* refers to what happens when a group meets. It is possible to change program structure to be more inclusive, but the values of the people who participate will stay the same if attitudes that everyone should conform to "our" standards are not examined.

A time of cultural transition is a good time to engage in an evaluation of the moral and social values operative in various facets of church programs. Members in many congregations already know that traditional programs are not working the way they once did. The people need direction from their pastor to lead them in theological reflection about the values they associate with church programs. As they attempt to revitalize old programs or add new programs, questions should be asked about each one in turn.

An honest appraisal of satisfaction and dissatisfaction with present programs is a way to help the people see what ideals control their hopes for themselves and for the congregation. Gathering factual information about who does what, when, where, and why is needed to correct a lack of information or congregational myths about church programs.

It could be a waste of time and energy for a congregation to undertake new programs and design them without an informed understanding of present congregational realities. An honest appraisal of the whole life of the congregation is a necessary preliminary to making any changes in the activities of a congregation. Once that has been accomplished, planners and leaders are ready for theological reflection about the future.

By including teachers, leaders of organizations, and people who chair committees in an evaluation of the program structure of the congregation, the pastor can equip these persons for their ministry. As leaders evaluate the activities with which they are involved, they can also clarify and discover their gifts for ministry. The purpose of program evaluation is to get an idea of the extent to which present programs contribute in a positive way to the faith formation and commitments of participants.

The following questions can be applied to any kind of church program and to its participants and leaders.

- What do we hope will happen in the lives of those who participate in this program?
- How do we expect this to happen?
- How well do both form and content contribute to positive faith formation for group members and leaders?

Leaders can ask if their present activities are a good use of their gifts for ministry at this time in their lives. As the leader of leaders in the congregation, a pastor can ask the same questions of his or her ministry.

*Hope for an Inclusive Family Pew*

Change in the family is not, as some have suggested, the end of the family. Families are a human necessity, a social institution found in all cultures in some form. Change in the family may be experienced as the end of "the Christian home" because family values have been so closely related to religion in the United States.

This connection between church and family has been more pronounced among Protestants than Catholics because of differences in theology. Catholic theology of the church makes it impossible to imagine that a parent as a priest in "the Christian home" could be more important to the faith of children than the church. Although Catholic families participate in religious rituals at home, the Catholic family is regarded as an extension of the church. The Protestant reference to the family as "a little church" can lead, in practice, to the church being regarded as an extension of "the Christian home."

The way a pastor leads a congregation reflects the beliefs and values associated with a particular theological tradition. Pastors are no less likely to be influenced by the family loyalties of the Protestant tradition than members of their congregations. Preparation for ordination usually requires pastors to study church history, Bible, and theology so that they will avoid uncritical repetition of the past.

Ideally, a pastor should be able to direct the life of a congregation so that members can be reflective about their values in relation to faith in Jesus Christ. Most Protestants would agree that an important characteristic of faith in Jesus Christ is found in acts of love of God and neighbor. But old-line Protestants in the same congregation may not agree about who is considered a neighbor, or what it means to love your neighbor.

The idea of an inclusive membership is not new to most Protestants, especially those who think of themselves as liberal. In some congregations, an inclusive church means that people of all ages are welcome at the Lord's Supper. Many congregations would say that their membership is open to all people regardless of ethnic identity. There are Methodist and Presbyterian congregations identified as "more light" congregations in which everyone is welcome without regard to marital status or sexual orientation.

Those who gather at the Table of the Lord on Sunday morning reveal the kind of people who belong to the congregation. A snapshot would capture the kind of people who actually feel welcome enough to become members of the congregation. What does that picture reveal about who comes to the Table, and why they are there? What kind of people are missing?

It is entirely possible that a stated intention to be racially inclusive is nullified and contradicted by the way members of a congregation interact when they gather. The act of saying that everyone is welcome may be an acknowledgment that birth into a certain kind of family was, or still is, an unwritten rule of membership. "Family pew" traditions and the emotions associated with them have influenced the way members have viewed the church for generations. If unacknowledged, the power of family loyalties can retard movement toward genuine inclusiveness because of the range of moral and social values represented by family commitments.

The biblical tradition affirms the family but limits its significance. An inclusive "family pew" is a gathering of Christians who worship because they want "to love and serve the Lord." Some children are there because their parents are Christians. Others are there because someone invited them. Teens and adults may have come initially because the church was their family tradition. Others are there because a friend invited them.

There are limits to the extent to which any congregation can be inclusive. This includes location and attitudes of present members. However, where members find an affinity with one another primarily because of family and class affiliation, they will find it almost impossible to see that "the brothers and sisters for whom Christ died" are the whole human race. Every congregation can be more inclusive if faith in Jesus Christ is *the* principle of homogeneity that binds members to one another.

In the early church, pressures toward apostasy came from "the world" outside of the young churches. Today they come from within. Contrary to popular opinion, the professed faith of the American people does not mean that the church effectively evangelized the culture. It means that the world is in the church. A reformed and reforming church is a vital force in any culture when her leaders are able to exercise their God-given responsibility for Word, Order, and Sacrament in spiritually responsible ways.

The church today is in no position to condemn the evils of "the world" unless members can do so with spiritual integrity. If the dream, identities, and behaviors of church members are not distinguishable from the American Dream of togetherness, successful careers, and upward mobility, the church in the United States can hardly offer justice to victims of cultural oppression. If congregations continue to reflect the racial and sexual prejudices of American culture in the way they define membership, authority, and power, the church will have very little credibility as a prophetic voice in God's world.

Leaders of Protestant denominations and congregations will be able to exercise more faithful ministry when they acknowledge the minority status of all Christians in American culture. A minority church is a church in a stronger position to protest establishment injustice. A pastor committed to service to a people with a different dream is a success when the people of God claim their unique identity as the Body of Christ called to servant ministry in God's world. Where there is hope for the church, there, too, is hope for a truly inclusive "family pew."

On that day, when evening had come, he said to them, "Let us go across to the other side." And leaving the crowd, they took him with them in the boat, just as he was. Other boats were with him. A great windstorm arose, and the waves beat into the boat, so that the boat was already being swamped. But he was in the stern, asleep on the cushion; and they woke him and said to him, "Teacher, do you not care that we are perishing?" And he awoke and rebuked the wind, and said to the sea, "Peace! Be still!" Then the wind ceased, and there was a dead calm. He said to them, "Why are you afraid? Have you still no faith?" And they were filled with great awe, and said to one another, "Who then is this, that even wind and sea obey him?" (Mark 4:35-41)

## EPILOGUE

# *The Servant Role of a Pastor*

T he letter to the Ephesians encourages a young church and its leaders to be strong in the Lord. This is a timeless message, even for churches that are not new or "young," as the first gatherings of Christians were "young." Every pastor and every congregation today can learn from the encouragement of the writer of the letter to seek unity in the Body of Christ, to grow up "to the measure of the full stature of Christ" (Eph. 4:13).

The vitality of the Christian tradition today depends on reclaiming the central affirmation of the church that Jesus Christ is Lord of all life. Otherwise, churches in the United States will only reflect the faithlessness of American culture epitomized in the attitudes and dreams of "the family pew." Otherwise, the churches of the Christian tradition will have nothing to say to religious seekers in a culture where people are free to believe anything they wish about God . . . and do.

In the earliest Christian churches, pastors and evangelists visited from church to church carrying news of the spiritual health of congregations. In times when the very existence of Christianity was unsure, this early ecumenical movement helped to keep the church alive. This was a way in which

Christians could learn from and give support to one another, spiritually and financially.

Few pastors today can count on spiritual support from other pastors. The Consultation on Church Union falters as denominations plan mass evangelism campaigns to increase their membership. There is very little ecumenical cooperation in a time when denominations compete for members. Within almost every denomination, money is in short supply. Departments, programs, and executives vie against one another for financial support for their programs.

Intimacy with God is normal in a congregation where committed Christians together seek guidance for their lives through Scripture and prayer. Today, few pastors will serve a congregation where this is a way of life for members. Rather, most pastors will face the temptation to conform to the culture of the congregation, to be shaped by the local tradition rather than to lead that congregation in new directions. That is why every pastor needs a friend in faith who is an "outsider." A friend who shares the pastor's dream for the congregation can provide the objectivity needed to guard against spiritual complacency or despair.

Every denomination has been influenced by the values of a success-oriented culture. Not many pastors will find support from their supervisors for a prophetic ministry that challenges the status-quo values of a congregation. The primary concern of most church judicatories is not the spiritual integrity of ministry. Pastors who are acknowledged and rewarded by their denominations are usually those whose success is measured by numbers of members and church budgets. This is what clergy talk about when they meet for judicatory meetings. As long as this is the pervasive ethos among pastors, there will be no spiritual friendships among them. These values mirror those of a success-oriented culture. Pastors see one another as competitors, not as friends in Christ.

In the cultural environment of the church today, there is very little appreciation for a Christian way of life. Fellowship, mutual ministry, and love of neighbor are not the values of a success ethos. This affects pastors as much, if not more, than members of their congregations. In a culture where the church has very little visibility as a social institution, there is not much social validation for the role of pastor. Where there is little cultural recognition, little or no support from peers, and minimal encouragement from supervisors, it is no wonder that so many pastors burn-out. Except for pastors validated by the appreciation of members in a congregation, people who respond to God's call to ministry today find themselves living a very lonely life.

Pastors are not exempt from the temptations of the American Dream—an idolatrous love of family, career success, and a high standard of living. The desire for success, defined by the size of a congregation, can blur the spiritual vision of a gifted pastor. Some fine pastors leave parish ministry in despair for lack of responsiveness among the people they serve. Others wonder if congregational ministry is their calling. Most do not realize that the battle for the hearts and minds of church members is being waged against the power of a civil religion that forms the life commitments of most church members. A life committed to Jesus as Lord of all life does not preclude loyalty to nation, family, and church. But it does mean a reorientation of the heart so that commitment to nation, family, and church are expressions of love of God.

Anyone who aspires to prophetic ministry in a congregation will need spiritual direction through friendship with some group or person who is not a member of the pastor's family or congregation. Although a pastor is called to be a spiritual guide and prophetic leader of a congregation, pastors need to receive ministry and spiritual direction, like any other Christian. Most especially, pastors need spiritual direction and counseling concerning their family life. The conflicting demands of church and family for the attention of a pastor creates tensions that can work against good relationships with their own family members.

A pastor may not give regular attention to meditation and prayer because of other, more immediate obligations. Yet, in order to lead others into faithfulness, a pastor must have some regular source of nourishment and support. Those who are called to teach and preach the good news cannot give away a love that is not real to them. In order to sustain hopeful ministry in both family life and the congregation, every pastor needs loving companionship and guidance from some person or group who affirms the calling and the person of the pastor.

A pastor who is not aware of his or her own spiritual weakness and destructive self-images will not be an effective leader of a congregation. A pastor who challenges the idols of American culture is not likely to find many supportive like-minded people in a congregation. This kind of prophetic ministry is not for the weak or the timid, the hopeless or the despairing. It is for those with a strong sense that they must respond to God's claim on their lives in this particular way—whether they believe they qualify for hardship service or not.

The leadership style of a pastor is a clue to his or her ability to act out of inner convictions about the church and ministry. Congregations with no clear congregational identity have been led by pastors who do not have an explicit, clear focus in their ministry. The pastor who achieves objectives through the political influence of a clique of friends is always in danger of being compromised about the focus of ministry. A pastor can avoid conflict by controlling membership on the most powerful boards and committees. But it is dangerous to pack committees with friends and allies, especially when there are clear differences in a congregation about the nature and mission of the church. If the pastor befriends only like-minded members, this will cause conflict in the congregation. Like any family group, congregations suffer from jealousy, envy, and "sibling" rivalry.

Pastors who can give focus to the life of a congregation are people who feel compelled to carry out a ministry that they know will not always please members of the congregation. Over time they are able to lead people with divergent views toward a shared vision of their congregation. In most congregations, creating a common vision of the congregation will take from three to five years. That is why pastors cannot depend on friendships within the congregation for support in a servant ministry. There will be times when their best friends in the congregation will not and cannot agree with their leadership.

Servant ministry demands a kind of spiritual integrity usually found in Christians who know what it means to wrestle with God with support from a trusted friend.

The pastor who can nourish the lost sheep in the church today will be a gentle spirit and an ardent lover. It requires patience, perseverance, and genuine goodness to offer new life to persons so that they can grow in their own way. *Goodness* means a spirit of sacrificial love that can see, appreciate, and elicit goodness in others. This attitude is essential to ministry that questions social conventions because it means that the pastor loves members of the congregation regardless of their present commitments. Pastors who love "their" people are able to see them as they really are and also as the more faithful people of God they might become. It means that the pastor is able to trust God enough to let the people learn the Christian life by living it.

A model of mutual ministry relies extensively on the ability of members of a congregation to minister to and to learn from one another. That is why the role of the pastor is described as that of an arranger or an overseer of spiritual growth groups. The personal presence of the pastor with each group should not be necessary if the pastor is giving adequate attention to equipping laity for their ministry. This assumes that the pastor is able to see the potential of growth in members and is also able to allow them to grow in their own way.

A pastor who feels compelled to attend every congregational event is acting like a parent who does not trust the children. Pastors who are comfortable with themselves and secure in their own leadership role do not need to personally control everything that happens in the life of a congregation. Pastors who are unusually effective leaders are good at training program leaders in a congregation. They are equally good at delegating authority to the many other people who carry out the agreed-upon programs of the congregation.

Of all the people in the contemporary church, pastors have the best access to the sources of God's transforming grace. Yet, like other people, many pastors have been formed by spiritually deprived churches. They may not know themselves as persons beloved by God. They may not have personal experience of what other Christians mean when they talk about "friendship with God," or of "intimacy through mutual ministry in the church."

A pastor can be a skilled professional in ministry, a fine theologian, a knowledgeable Bible scholar, and a good church historian. A pastor may be much loved by a congregation, may be a good friend, or may be a good counselor. But where the desire to love God above all else is missing, gifts for ministry can be misused. A pastor may rise to denominational, national, or international prominence. However, the career of a pastor who spends a lifetime serving unknown congregations in unknown towns and that of a well-known church leader come to the same end if they do not find spiritual wholeness through serving God.

The peace, the joy, and the sheer delight of pastors who are faithful to their calling is not the product of a successful ministry as it is usually defined by denominational leaders anxious to perpetuate their own power and position. The peace that passes understanding is not peace as it is known to the world of ambition, greed, competition, and success. Theirs is the peace of Christians who can relax with faithful service, sustained by a sure sense of the presence of God in good times and bad.

Pastors who enjoy their ministry are those for whom ministry is a spiritual discipline. They are people compelled to proclaim the good news in Jesus Christ because they have learned to see God's grace at work in their own lives. They are receptive to becoming ever new as persons through whom God's love is communicated to others. They can give and receive God's blessing as they lead a congregation into deeper fellowship with God.

Christians with an evangelical spirit, who are confidant of their calling and willing to take risks in leading a congregation into ministry are the kind of pastors who find members responsive to their leadership. Given positive sociological factors, they are pastors whose congregations do attract new members and growth; if their congregation is in a location where increased membership is not very likely, they do not have to feel they have failed. These pastors are not the victims of an ecclesiastical success ethos; they are not more interested in the quantity than the quality in their members.

Learning to lead church members so that they can grow up "into the body of Christ" may require letting go of the dream of pastoral success as it is commonly defined in the church today. It can require a prophetic stance within and over against denominational structures. Yet, the spiritually disciplined life of being a pastor has its own rewards. They are rewards not understood by the powers of the world. They are rewards not understood by pastors who have not experienced them.

There is no love quite like that of those who love and serve the Lord together. There is no commitment quite like that of Christians who are faithful to God and one another in the best of times and the worst of times. The joy of seeking new life together through the Spirit of Jesus is a delight given to those who sacrifice personal desire in order to seek the good of their neighbors. They are people who "know" the power and presence of Jesus among themselves. They are people who see the suffering Lord in the faces of all deprived and oppressed people. Such is the profound mystery of love when members of the Body of Christ reach out to God's world and move into God's future together.

# NOTES

## Prologue: Protestant Ideals and Historical Realities

1. For a similar analysis with primary reference to the Constantinian era see Stanley Hauerwas and William H. Willimon, *Resident Aliens: Life in the Christian Colony* (Nashville: Abingdon Press, 1989).

2. Robert T. Handy, *A Christian America: Protestant Hopes and Historical Realities* (New York: Oxford University Press, 1971), esp. pp. 214-21.

3. For a helpful discussion of nineteenth-century influences on how we think about "the future of oldline churches" see William McKinney, "Revisioning the Future of Oldline Protestantism," *The Christian Century* (November 8, 1989): 1014-16.

4. William G. McLoughlin, *The American Evangelicals: 1800–1900* (New York: Harper & Row, 1968), pp. 1-28. I agree with McLoughlin's thesis that all forms of nineteenth-century evangelical Christianity are permeated with "the ideas and system of the Scottish Common Sense School." Most contemporary "American" theologies are still influenced by some unexamined philosophical assumptions about how truth is known.

5. James Smart, *The Strange Silence of the Bible in the Church* (Philadelphia: Westminster Press, 1970).

## 1. "The Family Pew": The Church in Domestic Captivity

1. Peter Marshall, *Mr. Jones, Meet the Master* (New York: Fleming H. Revell, 1951), p. 155.

2. Ibid., p. 149.

3. This connection is commonly made by historians of religion and culture, and by feminist historians. For a concise account of the connection, see Neill Q. Hamilton, *Recovery of the Protestant Adventure* (Philadelphia: Westminster Press, 1983).

4. Colleen McDannell, *The Christian Home in Victorian America, 1840–1900* (Bloomington: Indiana University Press, 1986), p. 19.

5. Gloria Durka, "The Changing Family," *Religious Education* 83 (Fall 1988): 509.

6. Janet F. Fishburn and Neill Q. Hamilton, "Characteristics of Effective Ministry: A Research Report," *Quarterly Review* 9 (Spring 1989): 70-71.

7. Robert T. Handy, *A Christian America: Protestant Hopes and Historical Realities* (New York: Oxford University Press, 1971).

8. McDannell, *The Christian Home*, p. 106.

9. Janet F. Fishburn, *The Fatherhood of God and the Victorian Family* (Philadelphia: Fortress Press, 1981), p. 108.

10. Robert Wuthnow, *The Restructuring of American Religion: Society and Faith Since World War II* (Princeton: Princeton University Press, 1988), chap. 4.

11. Ibid., chap. 3.

12. Marshall, *Mr. Jones*, p. 152.

13. Catherine Marshall, *A Man Called Peter* (New York: McGraw-Hill, 1951), pp. 56-57.

14. Carl S. Dudley, "Using Church Images for Commitment, Conflict, and Renewal," C. Ellis Nelson, ed., *Congregations: Their Power to Form and Transform* (Atlanta: John Knox, 1988), pp. 99-100.

15. Wuthnow, *Restructuring of American Religion*, p. 31. The best evidence for this point is Wuthnow's study of the difference between the rhetoric of pastors about the church as compared to social realities.

16. W. Lloyd Warner, *The Family of God* (New Haven: Yale University Press, 1962), p. 266.

17. Jack Markum, "Membership Decline: Is It a Lack of Babies?" *Monday Morning* (December 18, 1989): 8-9. Markum shows that loss of members in the Presbyterian Church, U.S.A. is not due to a change in birth rates in the population.

18. Fishburn, *The Fatherhood of God*. See chap. 6 for an analysis of the prominence of familial language in social-gospel theology.

19. Handy, *A Christian America*, p. 220.

20. The Christian tradition has always been ambivalent about the role of the family in the life of faith. It has been theologically difficult to balance the tribal concept of redemption in the Old Testament covenant tradition with Jesus' challenge to this tradition and the imminent-return eschatology of the New Testament. There has been elevated love of family in other periods in the history of Christianity. This is usually related to use of covenant theology in which a form of Old Testament tribal attitudes about family have been uncritically adopted. Roots of family idolatry of the Victorian period can be found in the covenant theologies of both English Puritans and Scottish Presbyterians who emigrated to the United States.

21. Janet F. Fishburn and Neill Q. Hamilton, "Effectiveness in Ministry Report," unpublished paper, 1985, pp. 13-14.

## 2. "The Family Pew" and the Church Today

1. For an account of the mix of biblical imagery with patriotism in the thought of religious leaders and political figures in the nineteenth century, see Conrad Cherry, *God's New Israel* (Englewood Cliffs, N.J.: Prentice-Hall, 1971).

2. Thomas Charles Campbell and Yoshio Fukuyama, *The Fragmented Layman: An Empirical Study of Lay Attitudes* (Philadelphia: Pilgrim Press, 1970).

3. There has always been a tendency toward dualistic thinking in the Christian tradition. The dualisms described here represent a particular form of dualistic thinking.

4. Charles M. Sell, *The Enrichment of Family Life Through the Church* (Grand Rapids: Zondervan, 1981), p. 218.

5. See Janet F. Fishburn, "The Family as a Means of Grace," *Religious Education* 78 (Winter 1983): 90-103.

6. Horace Bushnell, *Christian Nurture, 1888*. Reprint. (New Haven: Yale University Press, 1967), p. 50.

7. Colleen McDannell, *The Christian Home in Victorian America, 1840–1900* (Bloomington: Indiana University Press, 1986), pp. 151-52.

8. In an era of hearty disagreement about theology, the Christian nurture of children in the "home" was one area of common agreement. See the review of *Christian Nurture* by Charles Hodge, a leader of the Princeton theology, in Mark A. Noll, editor and compiler, *The Princeton Theology: 1812–1921* (Phillipsburg, N.J.: 1983), pp. 177-84.

9. McDannell, *Christian Home*.

10. The inclusion of children in the sacrament of the Lord's Supper was recommended in The United Methodist Church and the Presbyterian Church U.S.A. around 1970. At about the same time the age of first communion was lowered in Roman Catholic congregations. The inclusion of all baptized persons in the Supper is new to Protestants though it has a long history in Eastern Orthodox tradition.

11. A similar line of argument is found in Stanley Hauerwas and William H. Willimon, *Resident Aliens* (Nashville: Abingdon Press, 1989), p. 10. Also see Stanley Hauerwas, "The Family as a School for Character," *Religious Education* 80 (Spring 1985): 272-85, for a similar analysis of the way this reasoning about the family in character formation "can too easily turn the family into an idolatrous institution."

## 3. The Effect of Family Idolatry on a Congregation

1. Some of the "border-line" denominations founded late in the nineteenth century by emigrants and blue-collar workers are more responsive to social injustice today than their old-line counterparts. However, the pattern of moving up in America is so strong that this orientation grows weaker as members become more middle-class. This phenomenon is seen in recent histories about The Assemblies of God.

2. Dean Hoge, *Division in the Protestant House* (Philadelphia: Westminster Press, 1976), pp. 83-90.

3. Carl S. Dudley, "Using Church Images for Commitment, Conflict, and Renewal," C. Ellis Nelson, ed., *Congregations: Their Power to Form and Transform* (Atlanta: John Knox Press, 1988), pp. 99-100. While this is only one of eight images described by Dudley, I suspect that the other seven include some allegiance to the idea of a family church.

4. Roy Fairchild and J. C. Wynn, *Families in the Church: A Protestant Survey* (New York: Association Press, 1961).

5. See Carl S. Dudley, "Using Church Images."

6. In *Choices for Churches* (Nashville: Abingdon Press, 1990), Lyle E. Schaller discusses these two types of churches in terms of church as community and church

as society. A major issue addressed in the book is how a smaller community-oriented congregation can attract younger members.

7. "Southern Baptists Condemn Homosexuality as 'Depraved,' " *New York Times* (June 17, 1988).

8. Donald Capps, "The Deadly Sins and Saving Virtues: How They Are Viewed by Laity," Pastoral Psychology 37 (Summer 1989): 229-53. Capps' research indicates that "our kind of people" does include a concern for ethics. He suggests that denominations are moral communities which see "sin" and "virtue" in different ways.

9. Warren J. Hartman, *Discipleship Trends* vol. 5, no. 1 (Nashville: General Board of Discipleship, The United Methodist Church, February 1987). United Methodist trends can be considered typical of other "main-line" denominations.

10. Ibid.

11. I am using *inclusive* as it is used in the church/sect typology of Ernst Troeltsch. His association of the church with inclusive membership and the sect with exclusive membership policies has been widely used by sociologists of religion in the United States. His typology is not directly applicable to religion in the United States because of the difference in cultural setting. The church, as he described it, is more like the established churches of Europe.

12. Jack Marcum, "Membership Decline: Is It a Lack of Babies?" *Monday Morning* (December 18, 1989).

13. Donald McGavran and George G. Hunter III, *Church Growth Strategies that Work* (Nashville: Abingdon Press, 1980), chap. 2.

14. For further development of this point, see Suzanne Johnson, *Christian Spiritual Formation in the Church and Classroom* (Nashville: Abingdon Press, 1990), pp. 81-86.

15. My suggestion that it is an act of prophetic courage for a pastor to serve as the spiritual guide of a congregation is not a metaphor or a "model" for ministry. It is a contemporary application of the historic formulation of the role of ordained church leaders as priestly, pastoral, and prophetic. From this perspective, I see administrative and leadership skills as acts of pastoral care for a congregation.

## 4. A Biblical Critique of Family Idolatry

1. Austin Phelps, "The Present Exigency in Home Missions," *Home Missionary* 54 (December 1881): 227.

2. Robert T. Handy, *A Christian America* (New York: Oxford University Press, 1971), pp. 3-9.

3. Ibid.

4. William G. McLoughlin, *The American Evangelicals, 1800–1900* (New York: Harper & Row, 1968), part two.

5. Ibid., p. 14.

6. Charles M. Sell, *The Enrichment of Family Life Through the Church* (Grand Rapids: Zondervan, 1981), p. 71.

7. Elisabeth Schüssler Fiorenza, *In Memory of Her* (New York: Crossroad, 1984), chap. 5.

8. See W. F. Flemington, "Baptism," *The Interpreter's Dictionary of the Bible*, vol. 1 (Nashville: Abingdon Press, 1962), pp. 348-53. Flemington concludes that "direct historical evidence of the New Testament is insufficient to settle the question either for or against infant baptism."

9. I am following the reasoning of Markus Barth that the writer of Ephesians, who is not Paul, is highly dependent on Old Testament thought and practices: Markus Barth, *Ephesians 1–3* (New York: Doubleday, 1974), p. 11.

10. See Parker J. Palmer, *To Know As We Are Known* (San Francisco: Harper & Row, 1983), for a critique of modern epistemology and an extremely helpful discussion of how "truth" is known.

11. Barth, *Ephesians 1–3*, p. 11.

12. Fiorenza, *In Memory of Her*, p. 270. "Although early Christian theology used this text from the Old Testament [Gen. 2:24] for understanding the marriage relationship, the author applies it primarily to the relationship of Christ and the church." In their haste to cite this passage as evidence of God-given patriarchal marriage arrangements, interpreters often miss the subject of the passage.

## 5. The Christian Life, Spirituality, and Sexuality

1. Although the single life is recommended in light of expectation of parousia, or imminent return of Jesus, this does not negate the effect of Jesus' sensitivity to the inequality of women on other aspects of sexuality.

2. William G. McLoughlin, *The American Evangelicals, 1800–1900* (New York: Harper & Row, 1968), p. 9.

3. Liberal theologians, evangelical revivalists, and Princeton conservatives were all fundamentally dualistic in their thinking about human nature. Neo-orthodox theologians of the twentieth century challenged some of these dualisms—though not uniformly—without much apparent effect.

4. A case in point is the treatment of masturbation in the 1970 United Presbyterian document, *Sexuality and the Human Community.* "Since masturbation is one of the earliest pleasurable sexual experiences which is identifiably sexual, we consider it essential that the church, through its teachings and through the attitudes it encourages in Christian homes, contribute to healthy understanding of this experience which will be free of guilt and shame" (p. 15).

5. In 1978 the Presbyterian Church U.S.A. officially condemned homophobia. This will make very little difference since the same document acknowledges that homosexuality can be a life orientation but declares that the sexual expression of that orientation is sinful.

6. For a discussion of four theological-ethical positions that represent a continuum in current theological understandings of homosexuality, see James F. Childress, *The Westminster Dictionary of Christian Ethics* (Philadelphia: Westminster Press, 1986).

7. See Darrell J. Doughty, "Homosexuality and Obedience to the Gospel," *Church and Society* (May-June 1977) for an excellent discussion of what Paul does and does not say about homosexuality.

8. Victor Paul Furnish, *The Moral Teachings of Paul: Selected Issues*, 2nd ed., rev. (Nashville: Abingdon Press, 1985), p. 65.

9. Victor Paul Furnish, "Belonging to Christ: A Paradigm for Ethics in First Corinthians," *Interpretation* 54 (April 1990): 151-53.

10. Frank C. Senn, ed., *Protestant Spiritual Traditions* (New York: Paulist Press, 1986), pp. 1-2.

11. Parker J. Palmer, *To Know As We Are Known* (New York: Harper & Row, 1983), p. 110.

## 6. Family-related Ethical Issues

1. This is the thesis developed by Philippe Aries in *Centuries of Childhood: A Social History of Family Life* (New York: Random House, 1962).

2. Ronald Goetz, "Picturing a Vanishing," *The Christian Century* (April 18, 1990): 395.

3. This information comes from *Pregnancy, Contraception and Family Planning in Industrialized Countries* (New Haven: Yale University Press, 1989), as reported in the *New York Times,* November 10, 1990.

4. According to a 1982 compilation of denominational statements on family and sexuality prepared by G. William Sheck for The National Council of Churches (unpublished paper) only four of twenty denominations said anything about "Single Persons and Sexuality." Only one, the United Church of Canada, raised the issue as to whether the church can accept a sexual relationship that includes sexual intercourse when marriage is not part of it (p. 55). The others do not acknowledge that this is an issue.

5. See Charles L. Rassieur, *Pastor, Our Marriage Is in Trouble: A Guide to Short-Term Counseling* (Philadelphia: Westminster Press, 1988) for a realistic introduction to the complicated dynamics of marriage.

6. "Clergy and Sexuality," *The Christian Century* (March 7, 1990).

7. See chapter 3, "The Single-Parent Family," Richard P. Olson and Joe H. Leonard, Jr., *Ministry with Families in Flux: The Church and Changing Patterns of Life* (Louisville: Westminster/John Knox, 1990). This book is the best treatment to date about how a pastor and a congregation can minister to a diversity of family types.

8. See chapter 6 in Marie Marshall Fortune, *Sexual Violence: The Unmentionable Sin* (New York: Pilgrim Press, 1983) for an in-depth discussion of why clergy assume that this is not a problem for members of their congregation.

9. See Charles L. Rassieur, *The Problem Clergymen Don't Talk About* (Philadelphia: Westminster Press, 1976). Although his discussion does not address the issue of temptations to infidelity for clergywomen, this may be the only book-length discussion of this "pastoral problem" and clergy marriage.

## 7. New Life in the Congregation

1. Eugene C. Roehlkepartain, "What Makes Faith Mature?" *The Christian Century* (May 9, 1990): 498. While I find the assumptions about faith as something that matures or "develops" theologically unacceptable, the information about "effective Christian education programs" is useful.

2. Ibid.

3. For examples of this approach to liturgy and catechesis, see chapter 1, John H. Westerhoff III and William H. Willimon, *Liturgy and Learning Through the Life Cycle* (New York: Seabury Press, 1980).

4. See Gertrude Mueller Nelson, *To Dance with God* (New York: Paulist Press, 1986) for a sensitive treatment of the moods and meanings of the seasons of the church year.

5. See Donald P. Smith, *Congregations Alive: Practical Suggestions for Bringing Your Church to Life Through Partnership in Ministry* (Philadelphia: Westminster Press, 1981) for examples of how to get started with this kind of partnership in ministry.

6. See Charles Foster, "Communicating: Informal Conversation in the Congregation's Education," C. Ellis Nelson, ed., *Congregations: Their Power to Form*

*and Transform* (Atlanta: John Knox, 1988). The essay includes a helpful analysis of the power of hidden communication networks in a congregation.

7. Robert Wuthnow, *The Restructuring of American Religion* (Princeton: Princeton University Press, 1988), pp. 52-54.

8. William T. Kosanovich, Jr., "Confirmation and American Presbyterians," *Affirmation* 2 (Spring 1989): 55.

9. M. H. Shepherd, Jr., "Didache," *The Interpreter's Dictionary of the Bible,* vol. I (Nashville: Abingdon Press, 1962), pp. 841-42.

10. Roehlkepartain, "What Makes Faith Mature?" p. 497.

## 8. Spiritual Formation Through Family Ministries

1. See James C. Fenhagen, *Mutual Ministry: New Vitality for the Local Church,* (New York: Pilgrim Press, 1977) for a fuller development of the concept of mutual ministry among members of a congregation.

2. Eugene C. Roehkepartain, "What Makes Faith Mature?" *The Christian Century* (May 9, 1990): 497.

3. See Charles Olson, *Cultivating Religious Growth Groups* (Philadelphia: Westminster Press, 1984) for instruction and encouragement to novices starting small groups.

4. See Herbert Anderson, *The Family and Pastoral Care* (Philadelphia: Fortress Press, 1984) on the effect of individuation/participation dynamics in the family.

5. For a list of resources, see *Parent Education: Family Enrichment Classes* (Discipleship Resources, 1987).

6. See Leila Hendrix, *Extended Family: Combining Ages in Church Experience* (Nashville: Broadman Press, 1979) for an excellent description of the house-church as a model for spiritual formation.

## 9. "The Family Pew" Revisited: The Church as the Household of God

1. See Craig Dykstra and Sharon Parks, eds., *Faith Development and Fowler* (Birmingham: Religious Education Press, 1986) for a carefully nuanced discussion and critique of Fowler's theory.

2. Eugene C. Roehlkepartain, "What Makes Faith Mature?" *The Christian Century* (May 9, 1990): 496-97.

3. Richard J. Foster, *Celebration of Discipline* (New York: Harper & Row, 1978), pp. 6-7.

4. See Kenneth R. Mitchell, "Pastor Luther From a Family Perspective," *Dialog* 28 (Summer 1989): 186-90. This essay is a good example of the way families in Luther's day differ from families today.

5. See Edwin H. Friedman, *Generation to Generation: Family Process in Church and Synagogue* (New York: Guilford, 1985) for an extended discussion of the effect of family experience and roles on the life of a congregation and its leaders.

6. For a helpful analysis of the changing family see "Children and Families: Myth and Reality," in Kenneth Keniston and The Carnegie Council on Children, *All Our Children: The American Family Under Pressure* (New York: Harcourt Brace Jovanovich, 1977), pp. 2-21.

7. This is one part of the argument of Christopher Lasch in *Haven in a Heartless World: The Family Besieged* (New York: Basic Books, 1977).

8. Herbert Anderson, "Christian Themes for Family Living," *Dialog* 28 (Summer 1989): 172.

9. Foster, *Celebration of Discipline,* p. 54.

10. See Maria Harris, *Fashion Me a People: Curriculum in the Church* (Louisville: Westminster/John Knox, 1989) for a fuller discussion of how to evaluate the life of the congregation.